MONASTIC WIS[

John Eude:

Thom... ...c...on
Prophet of Renewal

MONASTIC WISDOM SERIES

Patrick Hart, ocso, General Editor

Advisory Board

Michael Casey, ocso Terrence Kardong, osb
Lawrence S. Cunningham Kathleen Norris
Bonnie Thurston Miriam Pollard, ocso

MW1 Cassian and the Fathers:
     Initiation into the Monastic Tradition
       Thomas Merton, ocso
MW2 Secret of the Heart: Spiritual Being
       Jean-Marie Howe, ocso
MW3 Inside the Psalms: Reflections for Novices
       Maureen F. McCabe, ocso
MW4 Thomas Merton: Prophet of Renewal
       John Eudes Bamberger, ocso
MW5 Centered on Christ: A Guide to Monastic Profession
       Augustine Roberts, ocso

MONASTIC WISDOM SERIES: NUMBER FOUR

Thomas Merton
Prophet of Renewal

by
John Eudes Bamberger, OCSO

Foreword by
Jonathan Montaldo

α

Cistercian Publications
www.cistercianpublications.org

LITURGICAL PRESS
Collegeville, Minnesota
www.litpress.org

A Cistercian Publications title published by Liturgical Press

Cistercian Publications
Editorial Offices
Abbey of Gethsemani
3642 Monks Road
Trappist, Kentucky 40051
www.cistercianpublications.org

The work of Cistercian Publications is made possible in part by support from Western Michigan University to The Institute of Cistercian Studies.

© 2005 Cistercian Publications, © 2008 Order of Saint Benedict, Collegeville, Minnesota. All rights reserved. No part of this book may be reproduced in any form, by print, microfilm, microfiche, mechanical recording, photocopying, translation, or by any other means, known or yet unknown, for any purpose except brief quotations in reviews, without the previous written permission of Liturgical Press, Saint John's Abbey, P.O. Box 7500, Collegeville, Minnesota 56321-7500.

Library of Congress Cataloging-in-Publication Data

Bamberger, John Eudes.
　　Thomas Merton : prophet of renewal / by John Eudes Bamberger ; foreword by Jonathan Montaldo.
　　　　p. cm. — (Monastic wisdom series ; no. 4)
　　Includes bibliographical references and index.
　　ISBN-13: 978-0-87907-010-6 (pbk. : alk. paper)
　　ISBN-10: 0-87907-010-2 (pbk. : alk. paper)
　　　　1. Merton, Thomas, 1915–1968. 2. Cistercians—Spiritual life.
I. Title. II. Series.

BX3403.B36 2005
271'.12502—dc22　　　　　　　　　　　　　　　　　　　　　　　　2005010302

CONTENTS

Foreword vii
 Jonathan Montaldo

I. The Writer as Prophet 1

II. The Writer as Reformer and Author 16

III. The Restless Reformer 31

IV. Renewal and Words 48

V. The Role of Contemplation in Cistercian Renewal 63

VI. Contemplation and Recovery of Likeness 79

VII. Love, Transformation, and the New Man 95

VIII. The Nature and Meaning of Love 109

Acknowledgments 127

Index 128

FOREWORD

Thomas Merton's writing on monastic renewal in the Cistercian tradition is best appreciated by studying his ideas through the lens of his personal experience and character. The form through which he expressed his ideas is intricately related to his gifts as a person and writer, to the events of his life, to his relations with his abbot and his community, and even to the geography of his monastery. A presentation of his thought abstracted from his life is insensitive to the very point he felt was most important in any monastic renewal.

. . . [M]erton deliberately wrote about and taught monastic reform in a highly subjective and intuitive style. He is best understood when appreciated as a thinker who was a poet. He trusted his own intuitions, his own perceptions and experiences more than he trusted systems of thought.

—John Eudes Bamberger, "The Writer as Prophet"

When I read the manuscript of Dom John Eudes' conferences, delivered to the community at L'Abbaye de Melleraye, France, from August 30–September 2, 2000, on the topic of Thomas Merton and monastic renewal in the Cistercian tradition, I intuited its importance and hoped for its broader publication. Here were insights above the usual ranges for appreciating the *theological* significance of Thomas Merton's monastic personality as he gave it expression in his autobiographical writing, what Merton called in his private journals his art "of confession and witness" (April 14, 1966). To read Bamberger on Merton amazed me and was frankly a counter-intuitive experience. Here was a highly credentialed and deeply experienced, bleached-white-in-the-wool Cistercian monk and abbot, who had encountered firsthand the fissures in Merton's character, who was presenting his detailed case for appraising Merton as having been blessed with a *charism* for prophecy. Here was one of Cistercian America's most prominent and senior monks carefully explicating to a younger generation in Europe his conviction that Merton's literary legacy remains a cogent source for reflection and action in renewing lives of 21st-century Cistercians, Christians, and the world's communities of religious concern beyond.

John Eudes Bamberger entered the Abbey of Gethsemani in 1950. He was a scholastic under Merton from 1952–1955. He was a medical doctor before becoming a monk and later became a psychiatrist with the blessing of his Abbot, Dom James Fox. John Eudes and Merton worked together for seven years in receiving and evaluating postulants to the Abbey, when Merton served as Gethsemani's Novice Master (1955–1965). John Eudes thus enjoyed an uncommon and significant access to Merton and to his manner of daily observance. He knew Merton's quirks and idiosyncrasies, as well as Merton's intuitive genius for living the monastic life out of the variegated roots of his complex personality. Merton on occasion consulted with John Eudes on private and confidential issues, including matters surrounding a significantly stormy year for Merton in 1966. In 1971, three years after Merton's death, John Eudes was elected Abbot of Our Lady of the Genesee in Piffard, New York. He was elected for life and retired from his post at the mandatory age of 75. If anyone is qualified to provide an unromantic, critical assessment of Merton's monastic trajectory and what profit Merton's literary legacy might hold for monks and laypersons today, it is John Eudes Bamberger.

Thus the reader finds nothing secondhand in these eight monastic conferences collected here. Dom John Eudes takes his auditor beyond a discussion of Merton and the Cistercian tradition to expose his own lifetime's appropriation of that tradition. His historical treatment of the phenomenon of Cistercian "contemplation," and the role that contemplation played in Merton's life and literature, is brought to a happy close in two important conferences—"Contemplation and the Recovery of Likeness" and "Love, Transformation, and the New Man"—both of which convey the sense that we are hearing Dom John Eudes's personal and definitive reflections upon the contemplative life.

I have no special access to Cistercians to know if or how Merton's literature is being appropriated by them today. I could not make the case that Merton's literature is being received by them as still *au courant* to the existential realities they face individually and collectively, joined together as they are seeking God "through faith and fire" (a phrase of Gabriel Bertoniere, monk of Our Lady of Saint Joseph's Abbey, Spencer). I do, however, possess a layperson's intuitions, harvested from here and there, that many in his own country view Merton as passé for their contemporary struggles. He is for Cistercians today more a poet than a monastic thinker, by the evidence something of a "failed monk," popular it is true among lay religious romantics uninformed about the actual exigencies of Cistercian life today, his "cult" status tolerated as a "Sixties" phenomenon, but little understood: in general, for Cistercians Merton is an interesting literary character but, as a young monk might phrase it, "so yesterday." Perhaps this is a caricature to be corrected were I to take a survey on the question among Cistercian monastic communities. But whatever Merton's current reception among Cistercians, their General Chapter is meeting in Assisi, Italy in 2005, and is preparing to discuss the theological dimensions of the experience of "precariousness" in which many Cistercian communities find themselves. I would suggest that Cistercians have no better text to aid reflection upon the precarious nature of all human life and what a lived-theology of monastic precariousness might look like in the flesh than that personal testament bequeathed to them by their own Louis Merton.

He was a monk who consciously sought to live out of and through his always deeper questions as to how to be a monk of his times and summon all the personal integrity he could muster to seek God just as he truly was, paying a conscious price of demolishing any holy legend he was creating by his books. He truly sought God by going into monastic exile from easy answers.

Loyalty to his community at Gethsemani and Christ incarnate in human nature precluded his tolerance for the status-conscious institutional answer that ignored the needs and experiences of the persons sweating it out in prayer and work through every alternation of season and challenge in unique communities of persons traveling a common road at different speeds.

Merton was always *becoming* a monk: it was his work of the day, of the hour even. He kept himself awake to life as it was passing by in hope that the next moment might produce a wave that would push him further along toward the shore he longed to touch with his bare hands. Merton's journal writing over twenty-nine years (1939–1968), upon which Dom John Eudes places considerable emphasis in his conferences, can be received in their totality as an extended metaphor of the complex mysteries that attend each monk's life. Merton's personal testament to the need for courage and grace, as monks travel the twisted by-ways of their all too human lives, mirrors his wisdom that each human being is a developing "word," that is "stuttering to be made flesh" (a phrase of Canadian poet Leonard Cohen). This "word" always emanates from the heart of a life's progress. This "word" out of his own life is God's revelation to each monk. And it is a "word" spoken to the monk so that he might return it accepted and loved to God and to his neighbors.

Merton's conscientious exposition of the precarious nature of his spiritual journey, by wanting all his private journals eventually published, in a move he knew could ruin his reputation, reminds everyone of the absolute necessity of humility and transparency when teaching others how they might personally seek God. Merton's journals mirror to a reader the reader's own struggles with the mysteries of being human and alive in a unique historical moment. He reminds us that everyone's life is an ambiguous text that will contain mysteries to ourselves and to our intimates *usque ad mortem*. After Gabriel Marcel, Merton shows us how life as mystery is to be lived. After Rilke, he manifests what a monk looks like when he lives with force and courage through life's great questions.

Contemplation is the attention one pays to the complex (and very interesting) unfolding of one's life's text as a book that God is writing. God's text in us is first for us, but is also written for the eyes of our life's most intimate readers. Mindfulness that God is writing us into His Book of Life renders us responsive to His next sentence, His next creative paragraph in our unfolding story as we journey toward Him. Reading God's book, as He writes it, is an existential process without end. (In this regard, John Eudes posits Gregory of Nyssa as a major source for an aspect of Merton's lived theology of monastic life as attentive exposure to one's unfinishedness.) There is no Hollywood ending in the life of the spirit. No one achieves beatification in some static meta-reality beyond the human vicissitudes where we remain just as we are. Origen said it best when he offered the *sine qua non* for any real progress of human beings toward God: we must live in tents.

I recently emailed Dom John Eudes in Brazil where he was giving conferences at the Monastery of Novo Mundo. I asked him to answer two questions off the top of his head. "How would you characterize for me very briefly your own sense of the Cistercian vocation today?" He responded: "In our times the Cistercian vocation remains a witness to the continuing work of salvation in the Lord Jesus. The Risen Christ carries on His own mission of reconciliation and the transformation of those who give themselves to the Spirit of Jesus from their hearts. This is a lifelong work, an ongoing process of transformation of the whole of the human person. Creating a community that embodies a way of life that favors this work of the Spirit, and provides lifelong support, gives a social dimension to this work that is present to the Church as a whole, while it also provides support to its members."

"Do you think of yourself as a monastic reformer?" He responded: "I do not think I am a reformer, but hopefully a faithful interpreter of the Cistercian tradition for our times. I believe this characterizes Merton's work as well. Though my own contribution is a decidedly lesser one, I think it is marked by something of the same spirit and I remain grateful to Merton for what he passed on to me."

The author of a study on Evagrius and prayer, and most recently of a work on "Discernment in the Cistercian Tradition" that has been published in four installments in *Collectanea* (2004), Dom John Eudes Bamberger's conferences on Thomas Merton's role in Cistercian renewal is yet another important, perhaps an even classic moment, for a Cistercian master teacher to pass on his reception of the words of his own teacher to another generation. There can be no more appropriate place for this "word" from John Eudes, transmitting for us in his own voice a living tradition of prayer, than this number in the "Monastic Wisdom" series of Cistercian Publications.

Jonathan Montaldo
January 31, 2005
90th anniversary of the birth
of Thomas Merton

I. THE WRITER AS PROPHET

Thomas Merton's writing on monastic renewal in the Cistercian tradition is best appreciated by studying his ideas through the lens of his personal experience and his character. The form through which he expressed his ideas is intricately related to his gifts as a person and a writer, to the events of his life, to his relations with his abbot and his community, and even to the geography of his monastery. A presentation of his thought abstracted from his life is insensitive to the very point he felt was most important in any monastic renewal.

Merton's spirituality was essentially humanistic in its concern for the whole person in all dimensions: spiritual, psychological, cultural, and corporal. A fundamental guiding principle in his writing on monastic renewal was that any renewal should be less concerned with structures, abstract ideas, and programs but rather more concerned with the individual person. Where structures and theological and spiritual systems of thought do not serve the best interests of individual persons, they require transformation. When monastic usages become artificial and eclipse the work of the heart, they cease being true to the Cistercian tradition and must be revised. Merton gave explicit expression to this view in a letter to Fr. Ronald Roloff, OSB. He writes about changes in the Order at the time of Vatican II:

> It seems to me that here we are so intent on the changes we want to make, and the new possibilities in observance, liturgy and so on, that we are not paying sufficient attention to the *people* involved. In a monastic community, our first concern should always be concrete for the persons of the monks as they are, not abstract [as in concerns for] the nature of the observance and the physiognomy of a desired

new order. *Sacramenta propter homines,* and *regulae* also [Sacraments are for people, and so are rules].[1]

Merton deliberately wrote about and taught monastic reform in a highly subjective and intuitive style. He is best understood when appreciated as a thinker who was a poet. He trusted his own intuitions, his own perceptions and experiences more than he trusted systems of thought.

Merton's cast of mind and manner of viewing the world were in large part the fruit of his unusual education and early family life. The writing and teaching *styles* he adopted as best suited to his message were a reflection of his proper gifts, his personality, his character, and early history. His work, akin to that of Saints Bernard and Augustine, is formally more dependent on subjective factors than is the case with other monastic reformers who are known to us, such as De Rancé, and with other influential monks and scholars of our own times, such as Fr. Jean Leclercq and Adalbert de Vogüé. Accordingly, his thought and the style he employed in his efforts to influence the religious movements of his time can properly be understood only with an adequate appreciation of his personal manner, his style, and his biography.

Merton's gift was to write and speak personally but with great art. He himself understood this from his early years, prior to his entering the monastery, although for a period, after he had made simple vows, he lost some of his confidence in this conviction. Through a mistaken notion of piety he thought he should adapt his writing to the more conventional forms expected of a monk. The result was that he wrote in a mediocre style ill-suited to his gifts. The conventionally pious books he produced in the earliest period of his work as an author, while still useful, display little of his personal insights into character or into the movement of life that he excelled at reproducing in his later work. As a result they had but limited impact on monastic circles and on the public. When he produced a graph on February 6, 1967, to evaluate his numerous books, he rated

---

1. Thomas Merton, *The School of Charity,* edited by Brother Patrick Hart, OCSO (New York: Farrar, Straus & Giroux, 1990) 198–199.

Exile Ends in Glory and *What Are These Wounds?* as very poor and poor.[2] He later commented in his journal on his early mistaken notions as to how he believed a monk should write:

> If I had never written anything but the *Mountain* and *Thirty Poems*, I would feel a lot cleaner. *Exile Ends in Glory* continues to be read in the refectory, and people in general seem to accept it alright. Nevertheless, there are parts of it that make my stomach turn somersaults. Where did I get all that pious rhetoric? That was the way I thought a monk was supposed to write, just after I had made Simple Profession.[3]

It required some years (1941–1945) before Merton had full confidence in the intuition that led him to present the story of his conversion to the monastic life in the form of a very detailed autobiography. *The Seven Storey Mountain's* surprising popularity upon its publication in 1948 did not however prevent him from adopting a literary form ill-suited to his cast of mind in an academic work treating of the spiritual life, *The Ascent to Truth*.[4] He noted in a letter to Jean Leclercq that this book was an "unnatural" work for him. In it he was, he said, "trying to be academic or a theologian or something, and that is not what I am."[5] After writing *The Ascent* he learned to have a firmer confidence in going his own way. He learned by experience how important a personal style was for his life as a monk as well as for communicating the message of renewal of that life that he came to believe was intrinsic to his vocation. He was convinced that his abilities to articulate his private world were an indication of the way he could best serve God, could most fruitfully live and engage in writing what he believed was integral to his monastic call.

---

2. *Exile Ends in Glory* and *What Are These Wounds?* were published by Bruce Publishing Company of Milwaukee, WI, in 1947 and 1948 respectively. Merton's graph of his work has been reproduced in Thomas Merton, *"Honorable Reader:" Reflections on My Work,* edited by Robert E. Daggy (New York: Crossroad, 1989) 150–151.

3. Thomas Merton, *Entering the Silence: Becoming A Monk and Writer,* edited by Jonathan Montaldo (San Francisco: HarperSanFrancisco, 1996) 217–218.

4. Thomas Merton, *The Ascent to Truth* (New York: Harcourt, Brace and Company, 1951).

5. *The School of Charity,* 352.

Through his frankly personal approach to his work many readers recognized in him a freshness of sensitivity and a sweep of vision that they felt went to their heart. As Merton deliberately undertook to present his own history, his very personal, often singular, views and reactions, as significant for the Order, the extent of the interested public response surprised him. The wide audience for his work surprised the *cognoscenti* as well. Many religious professionals were unable to recognize in the public a spiritual hunger that the witness of a committed monk, who spoke a language that addressed their deeper aspirations, would satisfy.

As a Cistercian monk called to the life of solitude and hiddenness, Merton was quite aware that to publish his autobiography when still a young man and then his monastic journal a few years later, *The Sign of Jonas*,[6] would incite criticism. It was inevitable that he would strike some as contradicting himself by seeking notoriety and indulging in a remarkable display of egoism while he praised a life lived in the shadows. Yet he confidently proceeded to write his autobiography with the intent of publication. He obscurely realized, even then, that his way of perceiving his life would allow readers to identify with him in good part. He sensed that he could articulate experience in a manner that would lead others to gain insight into meanings and aspirations that remained obscure and unexpressed in their inmost heart. He implies as much in comments made concerning the spiritual influence of his life's story prior to its publication.

> Since I belong to God and my life belongs to Him and my book is His and He is managing them all for His glory, I only have to take what comes and do the small part that is allotted to me. . . . It seems to me there can be great possibilities in all this. God has woven my crazy existence, even my mistakes and my sins, into his plan for a new society. . . . Now I see what it is all leading up to: to the happiness and the peace and the salvation of many people I have never known.[7]

---

6. Thomas Merton, *The Sign of Jonas* (New York: Harcourt, Brace and Company, 1953).

7. *Entering the Silence*, 213.

Merton was 32 years old when *The Seven Storey Mountain* appeared in print. He had begun writing his life's story in journals at least as early as 1939 at age 24, two years prior to his entering the monastery of Gethsemani.[8] Thus he had spent at least nine years with some interruptions on his autobiography and during that time he maintained, though with varying degrees of confidence, his conviction that he had a prophetic, highly personal message to deliver to the world. He did not explicitly envisage his Order as a recipient of the witness that he was becoming for the people of his time, but in fact his autobiography had and continues to have a weighty influence on many Cistercian vocations. His conviction that he should write out of and about his personal experiences was portentous for the order as well as for the Church in various countries.

Merton was able, however, to handle the highly personalized nature of his work artfully with a view to aesthetically shaping the presentation of his experiences to communicate his ideas:

> Why would I write anything if not to be read? This journal is written for publication. . . . If a journal is written for publication, then you can tear out pages of it, emend it, correct it, write with art. If it is a personal document, every emendation amounts to a crisis of conscience and a confession, not an artistic correction. If writing is a matter of conscience and not of art, there results an unpardonable confusion—an equivocation worthy of a Wordsworth.[9]

These lines are fundamental for anyone rightly to interpret much of Merton's work that has a bearing on monastic renewal and specifically on his impact on our own Order. For want of recognizing how artfully crafted his writing is, many, including some biographers, have distorted Merton's attitudes to the Order, his community, and to his superiors among others. He is much more sophisticated as an artist than appears. Successful art disguises itself, and seems but a reflection of nature. It is that, in part; but a highly subjective reflection, as Merton explained to me one day in "the vault" where he had his office.

---

8. Thomas Merton, *Run to the Mountain*, edited by Brother Patrick Hart, ocso (San Francisco: HarperSanFrancisco, 1996).
9. Ibid., 271–272.

Furthermore, these comments relative to his "shaping" experiences in a journal apply as well to his letters, to his autobiography of course, and even to his works of a less autobiographical nature. He confessed the "art" in his autobiographical writing when he wrote of his method of producing *Conjectures of a Guilty Bystander*, a work whose final form often gives the impression of a collection of casual jottings somewhat loosely thrown together, but which is in fact the fruit of considerable art and much labor.

> I have been working on *Conjectures* in the afternoon—at moments it gets to be like Cantares Hopscotch—a crisscross itinerary of the various pieces taken out of time sequence and fitted into what? An indefinite half-conscious pattern of associations which is never consistent, often purely fortuitous, often not there (and not sought in any case). A lot of rewriting. For instance rewrote an experience of March 18, 1958 (entry of March 19) in light of a very good meditation of Saturday afternoon, developed and changed. A lot of telescoping, etc. In a word, transforming a Journal into "meditations" or *"Pensees."*[10]

In another journal entry he commented on the highly personal and artistic character of his writings upon receiving a copy of the newly published *Seeds of Contemplation* in March of 1949.

> Every book that comes out under my name is a new problem. To begin with every one brings with it an immense examination of conscience. Every book I write is a mirror of my own character and conscience. I always open the final printed job with a faint hope of finding myself agreeable, and I never do.[11]

He eventually made peace with his urgent need to put his thoughts and experiences into words and to write and communicate them. He came to see writing as integral to his life of prayer and his search for God. Already in 1956 he had arrived at a more peaceful acceptance of what he saw as a significant element of his vocation. Indeed, life and writing fused into one in his ex-

---

10. Thomas Merton, *Dancing in the Water of Life*, edited by Robert E. Daggy (San Francisco: HarperSanFrancisco, 1997) 297–298.
11. *Entering the Silence*, 287.

perience: only after he wrote of his experiences did he fully appropriate them; to live was to write.

> Either you look at the universe as a very poor creation out of which no one can make anything, or you look at your own life and your own part in the universe as infinitely rich, full of inexhaustible interest, opening out into the infinite further possibilities for study and contemplation and interest and praise. Beyond all and in all is God.
>
> Perhaps the Book of Life, in the end, is the book one has lived. If one has lived nothing, one is not in the Book of Life.
>
> I have always wanted to write about everything. That does not mean to write a book that *covers* everything—which would be impossible, but a book in which everything can go. A book with a little of everything that creates itself out of everything. That has its own life. A faithful book. I no longer look at it as a "book."[12]

I recently came across a discussion of the influence of style in determining the manner in which a message is received and acted upon that will, perhaps, point up the issue I am stressing in connection with Merton's influence on monastic renewal. In a work of history, *Sister Revolutions: French Lightning, American Light*, Susan Dunn compares the American Revolution of 1776 with the French Revolution of 1789.[13] She shows how the differing rhetorical styles used in presenting the ideas of liberty, equality, and fraternity influenced the sharply different directions the two movements soon took. Naturally there were many reasons why the style of the leaders of the two countries differed so much. The American leaders had practical experience in governing the local communities they represented. The French revolutionaries were philosophers without practical political knowledge to draw upon. "I dread the reveries of your Philosophic politicians", wrote Alexander Hamilton, American Secretary of the Treasury, to Lafayette. The Americans also knew how to accommodate conflicting party interests because of their prior, political debates

12. Thomas Merton, *The Search for Solitude*, edited by Lawrence S. Cunningham (San Francisco: HarperSanFrancisco, 1996) 45.
13. Susan Dunn, *Sister Revolutions: French Lightning, American Light* (London: Faber & Faber, 2000).

with opposing forces in their governments. They found that the most useful manner to achieve such harmonious accommodation was a moderate, gentlemanly rhetoric; they used the light touch. The French leaders, on the other hand, wanted every citizen to share the same sentiments. They valued above all else authentic feeling and were at pains to display this by a fiery rhetoric that considered compromise as weakness and respect for opposition as frailty. Opponents were seen as traitors to the cause and sent to the guillotine.

Dunne points out that language suffered as a result. "No masterpieces of French literature were produced during the years of the revolution. No gripping novels, no witty plays, no insightful essays, no great poetry." Bad style had bad consequences. "Inflammatory, hyperbolic, polarizing political discourse took on a life of its own and propelled events toward violence."[14]

After he had published *The Sign of Jonas* and had evaluated its manner of presenting the spiritual life, Merton had no basic doubts as to the direction his work as an author should take. He concentrated on his journals and on his personal meditations. The books that came from this approach were promptly recognized as the work of a spiritually gifted teacher and an original artist. *The Sign of Jonas* broke new ground for monastic spirituality in that it presented a day by day account of the experience of living in a cloistered community with the human and spiritual elements interwoven into a plausible account.

This very human manner of presenting the monastic life, treating as it often does of human foibles and trivia, seemed to the Order's censor scandalously out of keeping with the seriousness of Cistercian life and was rejected by the censor at first. The various letters Merton wrote to the Abbot General and to the censor present a rather vivid picture of how painful it was at times for him to be faithful to his original insights into the modern soul. It is significant that he began to have doubts that he was a real Cistercian after discovering the reaction of these monks to what seemed to him the appropriate and effective way

---

14. Quoted in the illuminating review by Richard Brookhiser, *The New York Times Book Review* (January 2, 2000) 11.

to speak to the people of his time and culture. But he did not doubt that his choice of genre was the right one.

> You had told me, in the form of advice, that perhaps I should not go on writing this journal. If this *is* your will, I shall not write it. But if you see no objection, perhaps I could pursue this very easy work. It is almost the only way to produce something with all my other offices, which look like obstacles. The publishers urge me strongly.[15]

Father Louis goes on to explain why he would like Dom Gabriel, as the General of the Order, to write a preface to this work, and describes the perspective in which he viewed its content.

> [T]he theme of the book is precisely the thirst for God which should be the very heart of the Cistercian life, and at the same time I present it not in ideal terms but in the concrete ambient of an actual monastery, just as it is, with its faults (though I do not dwell on them) and with all the charm of our Cistercian life into the bargain. A word from you would reassure the readers that the Order tries to look at things from a concrete and integrated point of view, that we have never deceived ourselves by pretending to be angels on earth. . . . I think, my Brothers in the Order—at least those who, like me, are not saints—will be able to find themselves in it.[16]

That this Journal was a major success and contained, in the view of Jacques Maritain, some of the best religious prose writing of the century vindicated Merton's instinctive judgment. It reinforced his reaction to the success of *The Seven Story Mountain*: "God has woven my crazy existence, even my mistakes and my sins, into his plan for a new society."

The other work from this period, *Seeds of Contemplation*, presented his thought in the form of his very personal meditations on some fundamental religious themes. Especially in its somewhat later revised version, *New Seeds of Contemplation*,[17] it has been considered a modern spiritual classic. It is still widely read

15. *The School of Charity*, 35.
16. Ibid., 35–36.
17. Thomas Merton, *Seeds of Contemplation* (New York: New Directions Press, 1949) and *New Seeds of Contemplation* (New York: New Directions Press, 1961).

by many laypersons as well as monks who find in it a modern, readable presentation of profound, basic religious truths.

As he continued his writings, much of which concerned itself explicitly with topics of monastic interest, it became increasingly apparent that Merton's role was to be that of a prophet and poet who, as a monk, lived in the cloister, at the margin of secular society. In his study *Heretic Blood: The Spiritual Geography of Thomas Merton*, Michael W. Higgins sums up the nature of his role as a reformer of monastic life and of society succinctly and with much justness of insight. According to Higgins, Merton was engaged in an attempt to "reintegrate shattered humanity." He criticized what he considered to be a culture that was in good part dehumanizing. He attacked current ways of seeing life. He attempted to set out a new vision of life, and to liberate the senses from servitude to encroaching reason by means of a poetic and artistic approach to thought and experience. Higgins describes Merton as an outsider who was at once a poet and a visual artist, as well as a social critic.[18]

Merton was by temperament non-conformist. All of these features signalized by Higgins are operative in his contribution to monastic renewal. Due attention must be given to these and other traits of his personality and style if we would grasp with justness of appreciation what he effected in the way of renewal and reform and how he went about communicating his ideas. These same characteristics noted in Merton are often perceptible in his writings in varying measure. They also marked the preaching and writings and lives of the Hebrew prophets. Fr. Louis himself realized this and, however modestly, understood his own role in monastic circles and his contribution to the modern world to be prophetic. He gives hints of this view at various times, especially in his letters. A few months before the end of his life he states explicitly, in a letter to Jean Leclercq, that he considered prophecy to be included in the monastic charism, though all too rarely taken up by monks. It is evident that here he implies that he understands his own work and his vocation to be prophetic.

18. Michael W. Higgins, *Heretic Blood: The Spiritual Geography of Thomas Merton* (Toronto: Stoddart Publishing Co., 1998) 4.

Thanks for your good letter about the arrangements for Bangkok. I will be glad to give the talk on Marxism and so on. Important indeed!!! . . . Those who question the structures of contemporary society at least look to monks for a certain distance and critical perspective. Which alas is seldom found. The vocation of the monk in the modern world, especially Marxist, is not survival but prophecy.[19]

The prophetic role has as its purpose such responses and results as conversion, renewal, reformation, and *aggiornamento*. All of these together represent the fullness of response to the preaching of a prophet. They are complementary aspects of a generous response to the inspired teaching of chosen representatives of God and of his Messiah.

Only relatively few responded with deep understanding to Jesus in his lifetime, and their appreciation of his mission and of his person was at best limited and inadequate; perhaps inevitably so. Until the resurrection actually occurred his work and its meaning remained more or less obscure. One of the major purposes of his appearing to his apostles after the resurrection was to instruct them in prophecy. He explained his life as the fulfillment of "all that was written of me in the Law of Moses, in the Prophets and the Psalms" (Luke 24: 44). Our Lord was very familiar with the history of the prophets sent to Israel and had no illusions concerning the reception that anyone could expect who was called to fulfill the prophetic role even to the people of God. "And so look! I am sending you prophets, wise men and men of learning. You crucify some of them; others you scourge in your synagogues and harass them from city to city" (Matthew 23:34). These words were addressed to the Jewish leaders of his time. They also applied to the generation immediately following his Ascension, and that is one reason St. Matthew records them: his generation of Christian prophets was also persecuted and rejected by the leaders of the synagogue.

The prophetic gift in its more public and striking forms was particularly prominent in the early Church and contributed considerably to its spread and its fidelity. Since apostolic times,

---

19. *The School of Charity*, 392.

however, this charismatic gift has usually been limited to a relatively few individuals. These persons were often uncommonly gifted in other ways as well as enjoying a special inspiration of the Spirit. Already in the times of classical prophecy of the Old Testament this was the case. Isaiah, to name the most gifted, was a great poet, a man of penetrating intellect with high connections at court; Elijah too was a man of tremendous energy and outstanding character. This tradition was continued in Christian times. Gregory the Great, whose works were considered inspired by the Spirit, exercised his great gifts of teaching, pastoral ministry, and administration in the public forum. The same was true of Bernard of Clairvaux. His endowments of intelligence, personality, and education, as well as the political sense he had developed from a childhood influenced by his father, who was a successful advisor in the service of his ruler, gave him a widely acknowledged authority. These gifts and assets were the natural basis for the exercise of his prophetic charism. His role as prophet was so significant a feature of his vocation that Father Vallery-Radot entitled the second volume of his biography of Bernard *The Prophet of the West*.[20]

Today there are many who consider that Thomas Merton was a prophetic reformer whose message continues to have social as well as spiritual influence in society. Among these are some of the best informed and insightful of commentators. Jean Leclercq, to name one, considered Merton to be one of the most influential of prophetic voices in our time. In support of this view he cited the theologian Hans Urs von Balthasar as observing that the most widely influential spiritual writers of recent times were monastics, such as Thèrése of Lisieux, Elizabeth of the Trinity, Charles de Foucauld, and Thomas Merton. In his study of monasticism in relation to our own times,[21] Leclercq cited with approval the words of Walter Eichrodt who, in a magisterial overview of the question, examines the nature of the prophetic way of life as presented in the Old Testament and concludes it applies to monasticism in the Middle Ages. Because

20. Irénée Vallery-Radot, *Bernard de Fontaine, abbé de Clairvaux*, v. 2, *Le prophéte de l'Occident* (Tournai: Desclée, 1969).
21. Jean Leclercq, "The Role of Monastic Spirituality Critically Discussed," *Worship* 39 (1965) 593–594.

they coincide with Merton's view of the prophetic role as it applies to our Order and monasticism in general, Eichrodt's words merit our attention, for they provide a firm Biblical foundation for Merton's position.

> By walking out of the circle in which they had lived hitherto, by making palpable, both in their dress and in their living a secluded way of life in special colonies, their opposition to any kind of comfortable worldliness or cultivation of self interest, so that they might dedicate themselves utterly to the religious idea, they brought home once more with unmistakable severity to a nation that had become too flabby and soft, that "life is not the highest good," and that there is something greater than earthly progress and the enjoyment and multiplication of worldly goods.[22]

Jean Leclercq himself is of the view that Merton's role in monastic history places him alongside such prophetic monks as St. Jerome, St. Peter Damian, St. Bernard, and Paul Giustiniani. As an illustration of Merton's witness, he cites a passage from a Merton article, "Symbolism" published in 1965:

> But one thing is certain, if the contemplative, the monk, the priest, the poet merely forsake their vestiges of wisdom and join in the triumphant empty-handed crowing of advertising men and engineers of opinion, then there is nothing left in store for us but total madness.[23]

This is but a single instance of many such texts that are properly prophetic in that they reaffirm the contemporary validity of monastic life and point to the essential contribution made by a life of wisdom and contemplation.

As we shall see subsequently, there are many sound reasons for ascribing a prophetic role to Merton in relation to monastic life. But his influence does not stop there: he has had a large effect beyond the cloister and continues to fill an important reforming function in regard to the whole Church. In fact,

---

22. Walter Echrodt, *Theology of the Old Testament*, translated by J. A. Baker (Philadelphia: Westminster Press, 1961) 326f.
23. "The Role of Monastic Spirituality Critically Discussed," 593.

as is evident from the list of prophetic critics and reformers Fr. Leclercq singles out as being the most prominent in monastic history, each, including Merton, has exercised an influence that went far beyond monastic circles. As witness to this wider and prophetic influence is the statement of the popular author Kathleen Norris in her foreword to *The Springs of Contemplation* in 1992.

> I find it refreshing, when reading this rough cut gem of a book, that back in the late 1960s, as Thomas Merton wrestled with what it could mean for monastic people to be prophetic in the world, he was himself being prophetic, saying what we need to hear now at the close of this chaotic century. . . . Merton reveals a considerable prescience with regard to the way in which a celebrity culture comes to trivialize everything.[24]

The Springs of Contemplation is a transcription of audiotapes of a series of retreat conferences given to contemplative women shortly before Merton's death. In one conference, "The Contemplative Life as Prophetic Vocation," Fr. Louis offers a very shrewd and penetrating analysis of American culture and politics today. This conference is an instance of Merton's uncommon ability to go to the heart of social issues and read the signs of the times that remain so obscure to most. He finds the key to understanding the totalitarian functioning of American society by discerning the ubiquitous penetration of profit and marketing in public life. Advertising reduces freedom to the pseudo-choice of brands of possessions to be acquired. Even dissent is co-opted and allowed for within predetermined limits. Words become emptied of meaning. What words signify is presented on the same moral level as its opposite. On page one is a nun with a new habit; on page two a half-dressed burlesque queen. No moral comment distinguishes the significance of the one from the other. This situation calls for a prophetic response. There is no space here to discuss the whole of Merton's perceptive treatment of the prophetic reaction to this alienating culture.

24. Thomas Merton, *The Springs of Contemplation*, edited by Jane Marie Richardson, foreword by Kathleen Norris (New York: Farrar, Straus and Giroux, 1992) 6.

Thomas Merton is the most widely read monastic writer since St. Bernard. In terms of the number of readers he is surely the monk whose writings have reached the broadest audience at any one time in the history of the Church. His works have been translated into twenty-eight languages and are read chiefly because of their appeal to the life of serious prayer and contemplation. Martin Luther, to be sure, was a monk and has had enormous influence that continues to this day, but his writings are those of a monk who had rejected his monastic life and even denied and attacked its values. Merton, on the other hand, remained an enthusiastic monk to the end of his days and his most popular work, *The Seven Storey Mountain*, is the story of a man's conversion from sin to a life totally dedicated to the search for God precisely as a Cistercian monk. His autobiography remains today one of the most readable and appealing presentations of the meaning of the Cistercian life for those who are unfamiliar with the Church and with monasticism. For the story it tells exemplifies God's merciful Providence operating in a man formed by the materialistic society of the twentieth century. The dominant theme in this work is not the person of Thomas Merton whose life it recounts, but the active intervention and guidance of divine grace in his life, a witness to God's intent of salvation for everyone. This theme is essentially prophetic and Merton, in this sense, was surely a prophet to his Order and to his time.

II. THE WRITER AS REFORMER AND AUTHOR

From its inception our Cistercian Order has recognized and honored prophets and wise men. The monks who constituted the first Cistercian community of the New Monastery were themselves prophets. They were endowed with the gift of wisdom in its contemplative dimension and in practical matters. They witnessed, first by their words and later by their manner of life, to the transcendent holiness of God. They established a community that gave concrete expression to their vision of God's holiness and persevered through years of testing to the end. The three founders, Robert, Alberic, and Stephen were not only endowed with the gift of prophecy but were each wise and learned, each in his own specific fashion and measure. They were perceptive enough to recognize the signs of their times. Convinced that God acted in them, they confronted those who resisted their message with great courage and persistence. St. Bernard, who was formed in their spirit, carried these virtues to an even higher degree, taking up their prophetic mantle. He carried forward their witness and unfolded the latent content of their inspired work. He disseminated their message by his words and works, which were often accompanied by marvelous conversions and miraculous testimonies to the divine nature of his mission. While this prophetic tradition in the Order has never been forgotten, it proved to be beyond the power of later generations to sustain it intact at the same high level of spirituality. The gift of prophecy among Cistercians has always appealed as an ideal.

Thomas Merton contended that bearing prophetic witness to the transcendent holiness of God continues to be a major function of all Cistercian communities true to their vocation. At the same time, he was increasingly convinced, as he gained pastoral experience working with the junior professed first and then with the novices, that our prophetic role was compromised by the functioning of certain structures of the Order and by a lack of adequate familiarity with the best of the Cistercian tradition. For the prophetic role to be refurbished changes were required. Merton studied the Desert Fathers seriously, as had St. Bernard and William of St. Thierry, among others, before him. He published his translation of their *apothegmata*[25] and used their words as a stimulus to prayer. He realized that to maintain a prophetic role for monasticism does not imply that all monks have those special gifts that the writing prophets enjoyed. He appreciated that already in early times there were also prophetic figures whose role in the Church was more ordinary and, while not hidden, was restricted to a relatively small circle. We observe this phenomenon especially in the monastic circles of Egypt in the fourth to seventh centuries. Younger monks who found themselves subject to perplexities or disturbing temptations regularly sought a word of counsel or encouragement from an elder of acknowledged holiness. Often enough they were persuaded that these men were passing on a word they received directly from the Spirit in view of their spiritual good. This would seem to be, in many instances at any rate, a form of prophecy. That the monks of that period were persuaded this was the case resulted in these responses being collected and preserved in writing under the title of "Sayings of the Fathers." Certainly not all the stories and sayings gathered in these collections are prophetic but a good number were so considered and with good reason. Taken as a whole, then, Egyptian monasticism certainly fulfilled a prophetic role.

No doubt many spiritual fathers and mothers, abbots, abbesses, and hermits, whose words have not been preserved, spoke and advised others under the influence of the prophetic charism that has never been lacking to the Church. Every monk has a charism for living his vocation, as St. Basil maintained. Few of us, nonetheless, would lay claim to a personal prophetic gift. Yet, by supporting one another in living our monastic call

---

25. Thomas Merton, *The Wisdom of the Desert* (New York: New Directions, 1968).

and by accepting the witness and teaching of the more gifted among us, some of whom, like Fr. Louis, may have a special prophetic charism, we can share in their contribution to the renewal of the Order and to some extent of the Church.

Our living together in the monastery is a prophetic sign in that our common life witnesses to God's revelation and proclaims by its life of faith that Christ even now lives and sanctifies for himself and the Father a people set apart. Like the prophets of old, monks cannot expect always to be listened to or have their example followed. But some, a remnant perhaps, do hear and take to heart the need for conversion so as to prepare the way of the Lord. As a community and an Order fervent in its dedication to seeking and praising God, a particular group of monks may exercise a far-reaching, decisive influence on others. This influence is not limited to visitors and retreatants but to others who learn of the monastic witness through those with whom they have had direct contact.

Merton was persuaded that bearing witness to the transcendent God by their manner of life is the major role of the monk in today's world. Whether preaching such a message is strictly a gift of prophecy can be disputed perhaps. Certainly a case can be made that witnessing to this truth today is counter cultural. Intending to live life fully in accord with God's law is precisely the kind of service undertaken by the prophets in Israel and in the early Church. After all, the greatest of the Old Testament prophets, John the Baptist, was viewed as a monk in his manner of life and is the patron of monks. Merton in a poem refers to John as "the first Cistercian and the greatest Trappist." [26]

Just a few weeks before his death, Merton gave an address in Calcutta, the transcript of which concludes with the following prophet-like statement:

> It is the peculiar office of the monk in the modern world to keep alive the contemplative experience and to keep the way open for modern technological man to recover the integrity of his own inner depths. [27]

---

26. "St. John Baptist," *The Collected Poems of Thomas Merton*, 126.
27. *The Asian Journal of Thomas Merton* (New York: New Directions, 1973) 317.

That Merton had received special gifts and had built into his character some qualities that are typical of the prophet emerged early in his life. Already by the time he was fifteen years old he had made his mark among his classmates as "something of a rebel." Fifty years before women were enrolled in the Oakam School, for example, he advocated admitting them. Before he had entered the monastery, aged 26, he had become, in the words of the headmaster of Oakam "something of a legendary figure" for the alumni who had known him during his early school years. He was so convinced that his way of understanding his life and the events that made it what it was held a prophetic message for his times that he had already begun to write his own biography as a layman, at the age of 24. He was convinced that his life story would be read by contemporaries as a pattern of God's ways of mercy and be a source of spiritual help. With the encouragement of his abbot he took up the work again and saw it through to publication. He thus became the first monk in our Order to make use of the autobiographical genre that St. Augustine had made so well known in his *Confessions*. The book became an immediate best seller. After 55 years it is still in print.

Merton was to reveal the same superior sensitivity to the spirit of the times in later life as a monk when he was among the first to predict the race violence in the United States. Similarly, he foresaw and denounced well in advance of others in our country the futility and immorality of methods that would lead to the disastrous consequences of the Vietnam war. In keeping with this insight into the world of his times, it is not surprising that Merton emerged as a major prophetic figure in the monastic renewal of the Order in the second half of this century. Later on we shall explore various aspects of his contributions to the changes in the way the Order has sought to interpret and maintain the Cistercian spirit for our times.

If Merton was a rebel, he was a relatively gentle one. He rebelled against those elements of monastic life that he judged to be contrary to the genuine values and aims of the early Cistercians. Merton had a strong sense of the authentic in nature and in human relations and a deep commitment to concrete reality in keeping with his gifts as a poet and artist as well as by religious conviction. As Monsignor William Shannon correctly observes, Merton was a rebel in "his refusal in any aspect of his life to be bound by a past that was static and lifeless."[28]

Merton was a conservative critic in the same way the prophets of Israel were. Just as they called for a return to the practices and spirit of God's laws revealed by Moses and handed down to their generation, so he witnessed in favor of the best elements of the tradition that were created and passed down by our holy Fathers and their more enlightened and faithful successors. This meant chiefly re-establishing a lifestyle that favored the cultivation of a contemplative prayer and of a truly fraternal community. This posture is observable in various connections, in his attitude to the liturgy, for example. "In the enthusiasm for new things I am afraid that much that is excellent will just be dumped for no other reason than that it belongs to the past. Then later, when no one can get it back, there will be lamentations."[29]

When Fr. Louis took upon himself the task of criticizing certain objectionable current practices and trends, and decided upon a far-reaching re-interpretation of the Cistercian spirit, he seemed to many others, including superiors, to be too liberal and even unmonastic in some of his views. This reaction is not only understandable, it would seem to be all but inevitable under the circumstances. Only someone with the same international formation, with endowments of penetrating understanding of modern society and values, and with an intuitive grasp of the more mystical elements of Cistercian tradition could be expected to appreciate his early attempts to modify the accepted practices that were identified with fidelity to the Order.

Merton himself in some of his enthusiasms and ill-conceived projects, as we shall have occasion to see later, provided at times grounds for legitimate criticism. Not everything he said and did was equally sound and, still less, subject to the spirit of prophecy. Often enough he himself was the first to recognize this and to retract suggestions he had made or reject plans he had conceived for his work or his personal vocation. He readily acknowl-

---

28. William H. Shannon, *Something of a Rebel: Thomas Merton, His Life and Works* (Cincinnati: St. Anthony Messenger Press, 1997) xii.
29. *The School of Charity*, 187.

edged mistakes and repeatedly admitted errors of judgment as can be seen in his diaries and in letters to his superiors and others. Any number of times he would be the first to discard earlier plans he had proposed.

In fact, while Merton believed firmly in his basic insights and his mission to communicate them in writing, he was very skeptical about much that he wrote in so far as it emanated from his own character which he saw as flawed to a considerable degree. He expressed a certain horror at the thought that he might become the object of a cult and taken too seriously as an individual. His message was given to him as a grace to be shared for the benefit of the Church, of society, of people who could appreciate his point of view such as poets, intellectuals sincerely seeking the truth, and those interested in contemplative life. He stated his attitude with his customary verve and self-deprecating humor in a letter to one of the Gethsemani monks studying in Rome.

> If there is such a thing as "Mertonism," I suppose I am the one that ought to beware of it. The people who believe in this term evidently do not know how unwilling I would be to have anyone repeat in his own life the miseries of mine. That would be flatly a mortal sin against charity. I thought I had never done anything to obscure my lack of anything that a monk might conceive to be a desirable quality. Surely this lack is public knowledge, and anyone who imitates me does so at his own risk. I can promise him some fine moments of naked despair.[30]

The fact remains, of course, that in spite of all opposition and criticism that he encountered, Fr. Louis remained unshaken in his basic convictions and insights as regards the fundamental aims of the monastic life and the practices essential to realize them. Neither the criticism of his Abbot General nor even that of the Apostolic Delegate, both of whom ordered him to cease publishing on issues pertaining to nuclear war and peace, diminished his conviction that the monk had obligations to his time that included social and political criticism when it was a

---

30. Ibid., 186.

matter of justice and charity. He obeyed because he believed in authority as expressing God's will, but continued to voice his convictions within the limits imposed by his vow of obedience. Thus Merton was rather a gentle rebel; he obeyed but did not agree and found ways to express, more or less privately, his feelings and at times his differing view. In a letter to Sister Dame Marcella Van Bruyn he refers to his own trials and struggles in a parody of an autobiographical text of St. Paul.

> I have had a lot of bother with my skin, due to some mysterious cause. And various other irritating things to deal with, which I suppose is all to the good. In perils from censors, in perils from (literary) agents, in perils from publishers, in perils from the Abbot General, by night and by day in an abyss of fan mail. . .[31]

If it is legitimate at all to speak of Merton as a rebel, the term must be seriously qualified as can be seen by reading the numerous letters exchanged with his abbots and the two Abbot Generals he lived under. The form his rebellious tendencies took was a refusal to agree with decisions and views that he considered wrong and, at times, to state his disagreement frankly, but respectfully. Often he also made his criticisms known to others, including writers and journalists and so embarrassed his superiors. When this would be brought to his attention he regularly apologized. I believe it would be difficult to find an instance where he actually rebelled "with a high hand." He would go as far as his conscience allowed, and at times, it seems to me, fell into rationalization when he was strongly drawn to some act or view that was contrary to the intent or even the express order of his superiors. This type of behavior, in my view, is not rebellion but willfulness, and was quite exceptional. He makes it clear time and again that he believed in obedience, intended to live by it, and sought to understand what it required of him so that he could put it into practice. But his insistence on pursuing matters he considered important and his frankness in expressing his critical views gave some the impression that he was at times rebellious. I know of no instance where Merton accepted such a

---

31. Ibid., 250.

judgment, and certainly there was never an instance where he persisted in a course once his superiors told him to stop.

The founders of our Order, after all, found themselves in a similar case. They too were viewed as rebellious by their fellow Benedictines at Molesmes though they displayed much concern to act according to proper form in all obedience. St. Alberic was even punished with imprisonment in the monastery for his refractory behavior. The disapprobation of their brother monks expressed in various manners could not, however, turn them from their purpose. They held firm and returned to their express desire to reform the community's lifestyle. When this proved impossible, they took steps to get the approval from higher authorities that would allow them to follow their conscience in obedience. They refused to be silenced or cowed into passivity and took every opportunity to pursue their project.

In fact, the reforming and prophetic role seems to call for a certain tendency to criticize the accepted ways of one's peers. Just as our founders had done, Merton also, after his earlier years of very docile receptivity to the teaching and example of his superiors, began gradually to revive his innate critical talents and turned them on those monastic ways that he considered to be faulty in light of the best Cistercian traditions. The young Merton realized he had a talent for satire and he cultivated it assiduously; it suited his temperament; the subtlety and irony of this form appealed to his quick and perceptive mind. Already when a teenage student at Oakham, where he was viewed by the headmaster as "something of a rebel," Merton's talent as a cartoonist was recognized and his satirical drawings were published in the school paper. He was also given to writing parodies, a specific kind of humorous satire. His natural inclination for this form of expression was abetted by his coming under the influence of his urbane guardian, Dr. Tom Bennett, whose example taught him that "perhaps the most effective criticism of all is a light superior mockery, the urbane and gentle murder of pretense and genius alike."[32]

---

32. Michael Mott, *The Seven Mountains of Thomas Merton* (Boston: Houghton Mifflin Company, 1984) 54.

Another trait that surfaced early in Merton's life that was to characterize his later critique of monasticism, the Order, his community, and various individuals was his tendency to exaggerate. As Mott observes, Merton regularly would exaggerate the defects of anything or anyone that he saw as the contrary of his current enthusiasm.[33] When he developed a liking for the Byzantine mosaics of Rome, he painted a totally dark picture of the Classical and Reformation art there. He himself did not take too seriously such exaggeration when questioned on it more closely. He could be objective when occasion or necessity called for it. But this characteristic misled some, who did not discern it as an element of style, into false conclusions concerning his real sober opinions, that is to say, those he was prepared to stand up for. Another of Merton's biographers has commented on this feature of his personality and style. "Throughout his life Merton was prone to extravagant responses, uncontainable enthusiasms, and occasionally intemperate judgments. . ."[34]

Merton was quite familiar with the Roman literary satirists and had studied their writings with appreciation. He was also a student of Erasmus who wrote effectively and famously in that genre. Of Erasmus he noted in his journal: "He is a splendid writer and to my mind a deeply pious one. And his satires: are they after all too bitter or extreme?"[35] Erasmus, like Horace, Juvenal, and Persius long before him, had found that satire could be more effective in curbing vice and human foibles than angry denunciation or overtly aggressive attack. To exaggerate and subtly mock the vices, stupidities, and miscellaneous foibles of antagonists has the effect of leading less perceptive persons to recognize them for what they are. Such a manner of presenting defects diminishes the influence of such behavior, making it less seductive. Satire has a way of depriving behavior of its sheen of respectability and reasonableness. So to describe the actions and views of opponents as to make them appear ridiculous and laughed at, markedly reduces their influence, makes following them less appealing.

33. Ibid., 68.
34. *Heretic Blood*, 28.
35. Thomas Merton, *"Dancing in the Water of Life,"* ed. Robert E. Daggy (San Francisco: HarperSanFrancisco, 1997) 80.

Merton, whose preferred *lectio divina* in his last years continued to be the Latin Vulgate, as he mentions in a letter dated 1966,[36] was also well acquainted with the satire prominently employed by the prophets. He read in the books of both Isaiah and Jeremiah mocking descriptions of the making of idols and their cult, and learned that the prophets were expert wielders of the satiric pen in the service of religious reform. He would have noted too that Elijah, long before them, as reported in the Book of Kings, also used mockery and satire in his diatribe against the priests of Baal to great effect.

Satire, to be sure, is a rather delicate instrument and lends itself readily to excess and the prejudice of the author. Under the influence of passionate conviction, of resentment, or even of high spirits and the desire to shock, a writer skilled in this form can pillory someone he views as an obstacle to what he sees to be genuine reform, but which in fact can be nothing more than getting his own way, or making propaganda for his personal cause. When the object of his criticism is an honest man acting in good faith, but, like the rest of mankind, possessed of certain limitations or even eccentricities, the result can be disconcerting, to put it mildly, to the victim.

Readers who are not sufficiently sophisticated in literary forms often take such descriptions literally, and consequently, are prone to form unfair or biased opinions of the victims of such treatment. Certainly that has proved to be the case in regard to a number of writers who have taken as literal truth or an objective appraisal some of Merton's satirical passages dealing with his superiors, his community, the Church, and some other individuals. In most instances it is easy to find passages that give a very different view of his victims.

Thus Fr. Louis's writings are readily misinterpreted and consequently used to buttress views that he himself never intended to support or even explicitly rejected. In addition to his using satire, being given to exaggeration, and regularly presenting his enthusiasms as contrasting strongly with opposing positions which he depicted negatively, Merton's style can be difficult for two other reasons. First is the fact that he was very

---

36. *The School of Charity*, 311.

consciously an artist with words. He wrote much of the time not as a chronicler or historian or theologian but as a poet and craftsman. He identified himself as an artist. He was very much at ease with artists working in various fields such as painting, sculpture, music, and especially poets. Now art is a highly selective form of expression. It is not subject to the same norms that apply to journalism, history, didactic literature, and other objective reportage. Art reproduces nature as interpreted and perceived by the artist. One day in the vault where Fr. Louis had his office, he showed me a painting of a landscape and commented that the painter had not attempted to depict the scene as it actually appeared in nature, but altered it in ways that expressed balance and harmony so as to bring out an aspect of it that appeared significant to him. The same is true of much of Merton's writings.

The second reason for Merton's style being subject to misinterpretation was his inconsistency. This feature of his style, both written and in personal conversation, has proven to be highly disconcerting and misleading to many. Merton was given to spontaneous expression of his current insights and enthusiasms without troubling himself about their bearing upon past positions he had taken and expressed. "Consistency is the attribute of small minds; genius knows no such constraints," he wrote in *Conjectures of a Guilty Bystander*.[37] Within limits, he considered himself free of such petty preoccupation.

I recall an incident that occurred in the late 1960s when Merton was living in the hermitage but gave a conference Sunday afternoons for any monks who cared to come. After a series of talks on Camus given with his usual verve and express appreciation for his writings which he considered important, Merton began a fresh series on the poet, Rilke. His opening sentence went something like this, "Camus is a man of the past and outdated. Forget what I said about him! Rilke is the writer who really has something to say; let's go into him now." One of the young monks came to me in considerable perplexity and said he simply could not understand Fr. Louis; he was too self-contradictory!

37. Thomas Merton, *Conjectures of a Guilty Bystander* (Garden City, NY: Doubleday & Company, Inc., 1966).

Michael Higgins has observed that Merton had a propensity to present his positions in contrasting, even contradictory, pairs. Properly to express his enthusiasm for Rilke he felt he had to downgrade Camus whom he had so recently praised for his insights and authentic stance before life. It might be more precise however to say that, because he had seen qualities in Rilke that stirred his enthusiasms, he now experienced Camus as a pale figure, limited and somewhat dated in his views. Merton himself was quite conscious of this feature of his thought and manner; indeed, it was a deliberately adopted element in his program as required by the genius of the Gospel itself.

> True holiness, faith, vision, Christianity, must therefore subvert his (Urizen, i.e., The negative influence of abstraction and objectifying) power to Negate and "redeem the contraries" in mercy, pity, peace. The work of this reversal is the epiphany of God in Man.[38]

Merton had been deeply impressed by Blake's conviction that "Without Contraries is no progression. / Attraction and Repulsion, Reason and Energy, / Love and Hate, are necessary to Human existence."[39] He called upon monks as well as poets to "dance in the clarity of perfect contradiction."[40]

Henry Adams had commented that "Children and Saints can believe two contrary things at the same time." Fr. Louis quoted this line, applying it to the English poet, artist, and social critic William Blake, whose work and life became one of Merton's models ever since he took him as the subject of his Master's thesis. Michael Higgins observes that the same capacity for holding together two seemingly contrary realities characterizes Merton himself.[41] Indeed, it was this similarity of vision in good part that attracted Merton to Blake. Such imaginative insight as is at home with contraries is not pure fancy or arbitrary juggling of ideas. It follows a logic faithful to a holistic vision of reality, having a respect for the imagination and the spirit as well as linear reason; it obeys the poetic logic of symbols and nature—the logic of life itself.

38. *Heretic Blood*, 74.
39. Ibid., 153.
40. Ibid., 159.
41. Ibid., 27.

It is not incidental that Merton entitled his Master's thesis "Nature and Art in William Blake. An Essay in Interpretation."[42] He was very much marked by this study and his involvement with Blake had a lifelong influence on him. He ascribed the origins of his entry into the Church to his study of Blake's life and writings.[43] Higgins is persuaded that it was due to Merton's assimilating much of Blake's thought and approach to life that "allowed his spirituality and artistry to cohere."[44]

Merton made a comment in passing one day in the course of a conversation, if my memory serves well, which provides a key rightly to evaluate much of his writings, above all the more spontaneous ones such as his journals and letters. "If a man regularly states his view honestly, as he feels and sees it at any given time, in the end it will appear what the real value of his thought amounts to." Merton was aware that this free and shifting manner of treating matters troubled many people as he made clear in a journal entry. He saw it as an expression of one of the most fundamental and positive of his character traits and had no compunction over it.

> I am aware of the need for constant self-revision and growth, leaving behind the renunciations of yesterday and yet in continuity with all my yesterdays. For to cling to the past is to lose one's continuity with the past, since this means clinging to what is no longer there. My ideas are always changing, always moving around one center, and I am always seeing that center from somewhere else. Hence, I will always be accused of inconsistency. But I will no longer be there to hear the accusation.[45]

Appreciation of the importance of this "principle" of frankness and honesty of expression unfettered by anxious concern for consistency is, in my view, fundamental for a proper evalua-

---

42. Merton's Master's thesis on Blake is reprinted in *The Literary Essays of Thomas Merton*, edited by Brother Patrick Hart OCSO (New York: New Directions Press, 1981) 387–456.
43. *The Seven Storey Mountain*, 88.
44. *Heretic Blood*, 28.
45. Thomas Merton, *A Vow of Conversation: Journals 1964–1965*, edited by Naomi Burton Stone (New York: Farrar, Straus & Giroux, 1988) 19.

tion of Merton's contributions to monastic, to his relations to his superiors, to the community, and to society in general. Merton was severely criticized by some for his frank approach to monastic renewal and spirituality, including the Abbot General, censors of the Order and some monastic scholars. He commented on this fact in a letter to Dom Jean Leclercq:

> Reflection on my critics once again: of course they have no trouble at all finding faults in me since I have frankly discussed my own faults in public. An *ad personam* argument is not too difficult under such circumstances. I would however like to see them meet me on my own ground. Let them write spiritual journals as frank as mine and see if they will meet the test of publication. I do not fear this kind of competition for I know it will never exist, or not in the camp of these amiable integrists.[46]

In a journal entry of 1949 Fr. Louis set forth this policy of frankness that had a marked influence on his style. This statement also gives insight into his spirituality and provides suggestive openings into his view of what he felt should be the climate of openness among monks for the future.

> To be as good a monk as I can, and to remain myself, and to write about it. To put myself down on paper, in such a situation, with the most complete simplicity and integrity, masking nothing, confusing no issue: this is very hard because I am all mixed up with illusions and attachments. These too will have to be put down. But without exaggeration and repetition, useless emphasis. No need for breast-beating and lamentation before the eyes of anyone but You, O God, who see the depths of my fatuity. To be frank without being boring. It is a kind of crucifixion. Not a very dramatic or painful one. But it requires so much honesty that it is beyond my nature. It must come somehow from the Holy Spirit.[47]

To many Merton seemed to be living a contradiction. He proclaimed, on the one hand, his love for solitude, silence and a

---

46. *The School of Charity*, 321.
47. Thomas Merton, *Entering the Silence: Becoming A Monk and Writer*, edited by Jonathan Montaldo (San Francisco: HarperSanFrancisco, 1996) 365.

hidden life while he continued, on the other, to publish prolifically, much of it quite personal accounts of his life, and to comment on current social problems. These contradictions, as we learn from Merton's journals, represented his fidelity to the obscure and often torturous way he was to travel to God. He knew that ambiguity and contradictory tendencies mark every monk's life and, in fact, are a feature of every human character.

The high ideal and transcendent goal of monastic life result in a tension that is at times acute. Merton was convinced that he could help others, including the novices and juniors under his pastoral care, to come to terms with their inner conflicts if he were to make public his own vulnerabilities and faults. He knew this gave his critics material with which to attack him, and accepted the anguish that caused as the cross on which he was to be united with the Lord. As the more private Journals published only twenty-five years and more after his death reveal, he carried this frankness to a high pitch of honesty, knowing his reputation would suffer in the eyes of many. Merton understood that to be part of the price for his prophetic and reforming mission to the Order and the Church.

III. THE RESTLESS REFORMER

"Today on the eleventh anniversary of my baptism I began teaching theology, scripture and mystical theology. On Monday I began a series of orientation classes for the novices."[48] The date of this entry in Merton's journal was November 16, 1949. The year before he had published the work that made him one of the best known writers in the United States, *The Seven Storey Mountain*, the story of his conversion to the Catholic Church and of his monastic vocation. He had been ordained a priest only six months before, in May, an event that, as he describes in detail, had a profound influence on his life of prayer. Experiencing Christ, the Savior and priest of all humanity, taking over his very self, Merton became intensely conscious of having a special responsibility for the whole of humanity.

> I am left with the feeling not only that I have been transformed, but that a new world has somehow been brought into being through the labor and happiness of these three most exhausting days. . . for three days we have been full of the Holy Ghost and the Spirit of God seemed to be taking greater and greater possession of all our soul through the first three Masses of my life, my three greatest graces . . . There will be no end to what God will pour out upon me, not for myself alone, but for the whole world . . . is it a fulfillment I do not understand.[49]

This experience given at ordination altered his way of experiencing the solitude that had such a fundamental bearing upon the whole of his monastic life, to the very end.

48. *Entering the Silence*, 372.
49. *The Sign of Jonas*, 193.

> Day after day I am, more and more aware how little I am my everyday self at the altar: this consciousness of innocence is really a sense of replacement. Another has taken over my identity . . . It is here, by the way, deepest in solitude and at the same time means something to the rest of the universe.[50]

Merton's work for the Order must be appreciated against this background of his broader consciousness of being placed in relation to the whole of creation and to all of mankind. It was the graces associated with the priesthood that stood behind his contributions to the reform of monastic formation and studies and to the renewal of the Order in general.

Even prior to ordination he had suddenly become the most widely read spiritual writer in the United States. He had a general sense that his writings and the meditations would have an impact not only on the monks for whom they were more immediately intended, but also for many others who were not monks, some, indeed, who were not Catholic or even Christian. He felt related to the whole of humanity, and, as he states in the text cited above, even to the whole of creation. This included the past ages of our human history and the future generations who would look back on our times for understanding of our age that gave rise to theirs. Later, in his hermitage, he would have a sharper consciousness that "the universe is my home and I am nothing if not part of it."[51] Events as they developed later in his life and since his death have vindicated this universalistic perspective that characterizes his work especially after ordination.

Such was the inner spiritual landscape in which Fr. Louis began the new phase of his life that involved the pastoral responsibility of teaching the junior professed and the novices. Just a month prior to commencing these classes he wrote a long letter to his abbot, Dom James Fox, treating of the subject of studies. Not surprisingly his views were not confined to the community of Gethsemani but included all the monasteries of the United States. This was more original than might seem the case at present, since there was no tradition of close cooperation

---

50. *Entering the Silence*, 327.
51. *Dancing in the Water of Life*, 212.

on the level of formation in our Order at that time. Indeed, there was very little contact at all between the houses of our country at that period; only those houses whose Father Immediate was an American would have any regular contact with a monk outside their own community. There was no talk at that period of such things as Regions; nor did one hear of a house of studies in Rome.

Dom James had already spoken with Fr. Louis about a program of studies that would insure an adequate, even superior training for monk priests who would be leaders in the community. Merton's letter was written to Dom James while the abbot was attending the General Chapter at Cîteaux in 1949.

> We should really organize our little seminary and make the house a center of really first-class studies in spiritual theology, especially Cistercian Fathers and mystical theology, with stress also on the canon law and other points necessary for future superiors. This really involves a sort of long-term plan. . . . The Holy Ghost really seems to want a center of spiritual studies somewhere in the Order in USA and Gethsemani seems the logical place . . .[52]

He goes on to develop at length the desirability of having a chapel where the students would be able to spend time in prayer. For those members of the community actively engaged in community service, Merton spoke of the need for a silent, solitary place set aside for their prayer. Eventually a large number of the houses of the Order were to adopt this plan, which seemed quite original at the time, of making available a hermitage or chapel for the use of those monks who could profit from periods of solitude. Some communities provide a regular "Hermit day" for the whole community on a regular basis once a month (my own abbey of Genesee has done this for over thirty years now) and some superiors (for thirty years I have done this) have a weekly day in a hermitage. Merton stands at the origin of this practice as far as I am aware. Certainly this letter is the earliest document I know of which recommends that it be allowed by the Order.

Some six months later Fr. Louis wrote another rather lengthy letter on the subject of formation, this time to Fr. Jean Leclercq.

52. *The School of Charity*, 15.

To him he described his hopes for formation of young monks at Gethsemani. He had made some practical arrangements already in the form of an expanded library to be available to those in formation. Prior to his time, and even for some time after, access to the monastic library was strictly limited. When I entered in 1950 the novices were not permitted to visit the library at all; the professed were permitted, if I remember accurately, only at stated hours in the week. He refers to his efforts to change this situation and describes his other plans at some length.

> We have just remodeled the vault where our rare books are kept and have extended its capacities to include a good little library on Scripture and the Fathers and the Liturgy— or at least the nucleus of one. Here I hope to form a group of competent students not merely of history or of texts but rather—in line with the tradition which you so admirably represent—men competent in all-round spiritual theology, as well as scholarship, using their time and talents to develop the seed of God in their souls, not to choke it under an overgrowth of useless research as in the tradition of the universities. Our studies and our writing should by their very nature contribute to our contemplation at least remotely and contemplation should be able to find channels laid open for it and deepened by familiarity with the Fathers of the Church. This is an age that calls for St. Augustines, and Leos, Gregorys and Cyrils.[53]

Few today would object to such a program.

I myself was a novice during the short period when Fr. Louis gave these orientation lectures to the group in novitiate formation and was stimulated by his class. He was full of energy and enthusiasm for monastic life and prepared his classes carefully. But the novice master made objections that having such lectures was against canon law in that it meant the novices were no longer trained by a single man who had responsibility for their formation. Having received this criticism, Merton recommended several alternatives, one of which was to drop the orientation classes to the novices and this is what happened. He continued, however, with the theology course with the junior professed, all of

---

53. Ibid., 20.

whom were destined for the priesthood in those days. Thus his first efforts were rather typical of subsequent interventions in this area of introducing the young monks to the Cistercian writers and Fathers of the Church. His efforts at renewing the program of studies for young monks was progressive and thus met with an uncomprehending and narrow-viewed resistance on the part of older authorities.

What were some of the features of Merton's program of studies for the junior professed? First is the fact that he did not mention the Cistercian Fathers as specifically as he had treated them in the orientation courses to novices. To the junior professed he stressed the great Doctors of the Church: Saints Augustine, Gregory the Great, Leo, and Cyril. These were teachers of the Cistercians, especially the first two. Thus what Fr. Louis sought to inculcate in his students was an acquaintance with the thought and the style of the Fathers in general. With an appreciation for the Patristic manner of presenting the Christian message the students would find the reading of the Cistercian authors much facilitated. They had learned from the early Fathers not only the doctrines of the faith but also a way of presenting them that was at once pastoral, moral, and spiritual. The spirituality embedded in the Patristic works included mysticism and asceticism, prayer, and practice. Since Merton's own style in many respects resembled that of the Fathers in being integral in its scope and intuitive and discursive rather than rationally analytical, he found it congenial to emphasize this study. In practice he did so with much verve and enthusiasm that the young found stimulating and even contagious. My own interest in Patristics, which I have taught for over forty years, goes back to his teaching and example.

As Fr. Louis began teaching and giving direction to the junior professed, he recognized certain traits common to a number of the students. In a letter to the abbot of Holy Spirit monastery in Georgia, he lists a number of traits that posed problems for a sound formation and were, in fact, exacerbated by the structures and dominant tone of current spirituality. Among them were the conflict between idea and facts, a strong tendency to force one's way to sanctity and thus produce strain and perfectionism. It turned out in the end that a number of the changes introduced by the General Chapter, especially in the Statute for Unity and Pluralism of the 1969 Chapter, were attempts finally to come to terms with these problems. In my opinion, they are much less common and acute at present than they were at that time.

One can easily make a case that the provisions of this Statute have led to difficulties of another kind. Merton foresaw these and stressed the positive: these difficulties would pose challenges to developing a more personal and authentic spirituality that gave greater scope for individuals and for the individual communities of the Order to respond to their monastic charism with a larger measure of personal responsibility and creativity.[54]

There are a number of specific projects that Merton devised at various times in the course of his efforts to provide a formation more in keeping with the riches of the Cistercian tradition. At a period when he felt deeply the difficulties of providing the kind of formation he envisaged within the actual conditions at Gethsemani, he proposed to the Abbot General in 1952 that a house of studies be made as an experimental foundation in the Rocky Mountains of Colorado where an estate was offered to Gethsemani.

> The more I think of the concrete situation of our students here at Gethsemani, the more I see that they need, temporarily, a very special formation that they will never get in the present state of things at Gethsemani. Why not take *advantage of this* estate in Colorado to send there a whole scholasticate, while bringing very good teachers from our houses in Europe. . . . Would the General Chapter allow in principle the temporary formation of a separate scholasticate that several houses would use in America?[55]

That for the last three years of his life Fr. Louis was living as a hermit in the pine woods about a kilometer north of the Abbey represents a major breakthrough in his efforts to re-establish the hermit tradition in Order. This has had greater sig-

---

54. Ibid., 58.
55. Ibid., 37.

nificance than might at first appear for renewal in the Order. It has affected not only the relatively few who have formally become hermits, but it has served to put in relief the importance of silence, simplicity, solitude, separation from the world, and asceticism for all monks. In his efforts to introduce the possibility for those called to this vocation to follow it while remaining in the Order he collaborated closely with his Abbot, Dom James Fox, who himself was eventually to retire after twenty years in office, and live almost another twenty years as a hermit. It was their combined efforts that brought about the acceptance by the Chapter of the hermit life and introduced it into our Constitutions.

In the course of this collaboration with his abbot for resurrecting the hermit life, Merton certainly took the initiative and displayed a remarkable degree of persistence, patience, obedience, and ingenuity as the rather long list of his letters and journal entries demonstrate. Among various tokens of his ingenuity in producing supportive arguments for his position is his pointing out that de Rancé had a hermit at La Trappe.

As a result of his patient persistence he was able to obtain at first periods of solitude in the woods that proved beneficial not only for his spirit but also for his peace of mind and his health. Some of his most revealing experiences of God and deepest insights into the contemplative life, some of his most enlightening pages on pure prayer that are now part of the Cistercian heritage, were the result of the days and months spent first in St. Anne's, a toolshed, then later in the hermitage built for his use. We shall have occasion to reflect more on those experiences when we treat of the contemplative life and of the process of transformation.

In addition to his prolonged struggles to introduce more solitude into the framework of Trappist practice, Merton elaborated a practical plan for living the hermit life while remaining in the Order. Entitled *Project for a Hermitage*, it was first published in a limited edition in 1960 and reprinted in *The Monastic Journey*.[56] This project is of considerable interest for understanding Merton's mature thought on the hermit life and is obviously

---

56. Thomas Merton, *The Monastic Journey*, edited by Brother Patrick Hart, OCSO (Kansas City, MO: Sheed Andrews and McMeel, Inc., 1977) 135–143.

based on a rather broad pastoral experience. Besides providing proof that Merton could be quite practical in his arrangements, it states the spiritual and pastoral rationale for providing the eremitical dimension of monastic life for members of the Order. The whole project reveals the earnestness with which he considered the place of solitude and contemplative prayer in the Cistercian life while recognizing the exceptional nature of such a solitary vocation. The following lines state the matter concisely.

> [t]he chief penitential emphasis would be on solitude and silence, on remaining alone in prayer, simplicity and poverty. . . . The great work of the hermit would be *prayer*. He would consider himself set apart by God for this above all. His prayer would take the forms inspired by the Holy Spirit, dictated by his own needs and the needs of the Church and approved by his Spiritual Father. His prayer would be supported by solid *Lectio* and perhaps also by some study according to his temperament and needs.[57]

Father Jean Leclercq, who studied the nature of the Cistercian tradition more than any other scholar in this century, observed that there is nothing in the Cistercian way that is not found elsewhere in traditional monasticism or in the new foundations. What constituted the Cistercian tradition was the specific choices made and the particular emphasis given to certain elements that were selected from the broader tradition of the Church.[58] P. Placide Deseilles studied this same question and pointed out how the Cistercian reform had no intent of creating anything new.

> The purpose of the founders was not to begin a new form of religious life in the Church but only to make the ancient tradition of cenobitic monasticism live again in all its fervor. On the other hand, the teaching of St. Bernard and the spiritual masters of the second Cistercian generation wanted only to be the living echo of the Patristic tradition.[59]

---

57. Ibid., 140–141.
58. Jean Leclercq, *L'Histoire de la Spiritualité Chrétienne vol. II: La Spiritualité du Moyen Âge* (Francois Vandenbroucke, Louis Bouyer, Paris. Aubier, 1960) 237.
59. P. Placide Deseilles, *Cîteaux et La Tradition Monastique, Christus* 7 (1960) (Paris: Les Perès de la Societé de Jesus) 128.

Deseilles concludes that Cistercian spirituality is nothing else than the common monastic spirituality that thus makes it the least specialized of all types. But the Cistercian tradition does in fact have its own characteristics. Fidelity to the sources of monastic life and to the Fathers of the Church has a special place in Cistercian monasticism. Olivier Rousseau designates this feature "historical catholicity".[60] He maintains that authenticity is a second characteristic, that is to say, the founders insisted that usages were not to be obeyed because they were traditional but because they led to purity of heart and facilitated union with God. Poverty and simplicity were emphasized with particular attention as well, and this included the liturgy. A final trait is the emphasis on interiority. The founders saw their life as a return to the heart where they encountered the Word who visited them in prayer giving a foretaste of heaven.

This is an important feature to advert to; it means that there is something very Catholic about the Cistercian heritage. It is not exclusionist in its origins but derives from a larger body of doctrine and practice that sustains it. It maintains many bonds with the spirituality and life of other traditions and vocations. Merton had a strong sense of this Catholicity and that is one reason his work for the renewal of the Order in our times has found such a sympathetic response by many religious of other traditions, including not only Benedictines but Franciscans, Carmelites, and Jesuits, as well as numerous laymen. He also posed the question as to the nature of the Cistercian tradition. He answered it characteristically, not with some academic or abstract formula, but by recommending a visit to a Trappist monastery! Here is Merton's description of the spirit of Cîteaux.

> What was the Cistercian spirit? What was the character that the monasteries of Cîteaux communicated to the world of their time? This Cistercian spirit is something that does not altogether belong to the past. . . . Those who are interested in the Cistercian spirit can form at least a vague notion of it by visiting a Trappist monastery, breathing the silence of the cloister, walking in the fields tilled by the

---

60. *Monachisme et vie religious d'après l'ancienne tradition de l'Église* (Chevtogne: Editions de Chevtogne, 1957) 170, cited by Deseilles.

hands of the monks, or listening to their chant in the monastic choir. The Cistercian spirit is a beautiful combination of ardor, simplicity and strength. At the root of the Cistercian reform was a hatred of artificiality and an intense impatience with the illogical compromises into which monks are led when they yield to the obscure enticements of the world, the flesh and the devil, and live like worldlings under the guise of religious. St. Stephen Harding and his companions were consumed by the passionate desire for truth.[61]

If we wish to take fuller advantage of Merton's contribution to Cistercian tradition, we can hardly do better than read his journals. Not only the ones published in his lifetime, but especially those now fully published in seven volumes, because they contain more intimate material, published twenty-five years after his death. They provide a window into his lifelong search for authenticity of life, especially of his life of prayer. His honesty leads him repeatedly to confess his failures with a clear-sighted frankness that surprises at times. This concern to live from the depths of his spirit, in the presence of God, is perhaps his most important contribution to the work of on-going renewal of the Order. One instance of many is an entry made on September 6, 1948.

> To make a Rule the whole meaning of my existence is not enough. To make an Order, a spiritual tradition, the center of my life is not enough. Contemplation is not enough: by itself it is not enough of an ideal. The complete gift of myself to Christ—transformation—total simplicity and poverty—these are some of the things I need.[62]

Merton's desire for the authentic, for truth, and for a radical transformation motivated Merton's concern for reforming the studies in the Order. In this he was acting from the heart of our Cistercian tradition.

On various occasions and in a variety of ways Fr. Louis made suggestions concerning formation and studies in the Order. He envisioned a course of studies that would make monks conver-

---

61. *Saint Aelred of Rievaulx and the Cistercians*, Cistercian Studies 20 (1985) 214.
62. Thomas Merton, *Entering the Silence*, volume 2 of the Merton Journals, edited by Jonathan Montaldo (San Francisco: HarperSanFrancisco, 1996) 229.

sant with the best of the monastic tradition as well as with those currents of thought and historical movements that were dominant in Western society. In 1967, at the request of Dom John Morson, the English Definitor in Rome, Fr. Louis wrote an extensive memorandum that details his guiding principles regarding monastic formation and especially a study program for the more intellectually inclined. These reflections are the most complete resumé of his views on formation and priestly studies. They depict his concept of the ideal monastic culture. It is obvious that he had in mind a community of intellectuals of the kind he had repeatedly considered founding, especially in Latin America. In practice, it describes his own approach to formation as he was able to implement it at Gethsemani during his years as Master of Junior Professed. As one of that group I can recognize in this document the spirit and much of the specific provisions as having entered in to our formation.

"A Memorandum on Monastic Theology"[63] deserves study especially for its specific recommendations. These furnish insight into his own formation as a writer and teacher. They encapsulate his vision, at the end of his life, of what kind of culture a truly modern Cistercian monk would enjoy and disseminate in his community and among those he contacted outside.

- Adequate training in the disciplines of an ascetic life and means provided by our own tradition.
- Open the way to a *sapiential* rather than *scientific* theology.
- Provide adequate introduction to humanities, in which modern candidates are poorly prepared.
- Training in contemplative theology that would include not only our own tradition but non-Christian traditions as well.
- A study of comparative religion with an opening to psychiatry.
- Theology itself deeply and thoroughly Biblical and Patristic.
- In order to understand our times, the importance of history.

63. *Cistercian Studies Quarterly*, XXVI (1991) 191–194.

- The social and political problems of our time: peace and war, civil rights, responsibility of rich nations to poor.
- A study of the world of technology and science in view of the monk making an eventual contribution to the spiritual wisdom of that world.

These recommendations do not aim at creating specialists of mystical and intellectual dialogue that would be a Utopian project. The aim is to form monks "who are capable of embracing in their contemplative awareness not only the theological dimensions of the mystery of Christ but also the possibilities of new understanding offered by non-Christian traditions and by the modern world of science and revolution." He allows for occasional travel from the cloister that would permit contact with currents of life and thought. Such forays would enable a monk to profit from experience in appropriate areas so that he might benefit his community and/or guests who come to the monastery.

Merton's views prepared the way for gatherings of monks from different monasteries to discuss topics of common interest. He paved the way for these now regular gatherings that had their beginning in our Order in 1969, the year after his death, with a meeting on formation by a group of monks representing the various regions of the Order. The recommendations of that meeting largely anticipated the provisions of the first *Ratio Studiorum* (a plan of studies) that appeared not long after. As a member of that Committee I expressed a number of opinions I had come to appreciate from studying under Fr. Louis. By that time and through other influences as well, members from other regions, notably Belgium (P. Maur Standaert) and France (Dom Hervé) held views that were conceived in the same spirit as Merton's teaching. The climate of that first meeting was warmly fraternal and the dialogue was frank and congenial, a fact that attested to a communion in the Cistercian tradition and spirit.

To evaluate properly Merton's contribution in regard to studies and formation it is necessary to advert to the program that was in force prior to the changes he advocated and introduced at Gethsemani both in the novitiate and in the formation of the junior professed. When he began to teach in 1951, it would have been an anachronism to speak of the juniorate for there was no such distinct, formal group with a monk charged to assist in their spiritual and monastic formation. Students were in a program of studies for the priesthood that was conducted along lines of a seminary. Naturally, the students were living a regular monastic life, even doing manual work half time as well as following the regular schedule that included about twice as much time in choir as at present. The studies were based upon the manuals of theology written in Latin and it was strictly academic and quite technical in style and origin.

The more literary, contemplative approach of the Patristic style that Merton preferred and employed in his own classes represented a radical change of mentality; indeed, it required being formed to a new culture. It was not merely a question of using different texts and authors, but of cultivating a taste for another way of thinking. Merton was teaching the employment of a different kind of logic, the logic of symbolism, of experience, of life itself. Such a manner of organizing material and of thinking can seem very untidy and even invalid to those formed in a more technical and scientific world.

After Merton had already begun to employ this approach in his manner of teaching the juniors for some time, he was confronted with the same problem some years later as novice master when the brothers were fused with the choir in the novitiate. In a letter to a Gethsemani student studying in Europe, Merton described the situation that he found in his usual highly colorful manner.

> It is just that nobody ever told the brothers that the Fathers of the Church existed, and that there was such a thing as the Monastic Tradition, and that it was alive. Tradition, according to the usual concept, is *ipso facto* dead. If you get it from somebody else it is dead. This is a myth and of course it does not stop people from running around slavishly imitating the world models.[64]

Since my own formation had been in science and was quite technical, I profited greatly from the way Fr. Louis was able to

---

64. *The School of Charity*, 174.

present theological and spiritual matters in a language that made their teaching more accessible. Already the orientation talks to the novices introduced us into this Patristic world. John Cassian in particular was a favorite source for Merton throughout his monastic life, and he knew how to bring his teaching to life. He refers to his lectures to his novices in a letter of 1955 to Fr. Jean Leclercq, for instance, which gives some idea of the feeling he brought to his classes.

> Meanwhile for my part I am happily lecturing on Cassian. What could be better material in my situation? Although I cannot live like Abbot Isaac, Nestorius, or Piamon I feel that they are my fathers and my friends.[65]

A few years later, in replying to a request by an American novice-master he tells him that "If you have not read Cassian thoroughly, you should. Also the *Verba Seniorum* (Desert Fathers). I am bringing out a translation of this latter in part."[66]

One of the most intractable obstacles that Merton, along with others in the Order who sought to effect needed changes, was voluntarism. This was due, in large part, I believe, to the fact that there was so little knowledge of the Tradition in depth that a large number of monks—and, as I discovered later, even more of the nuns, could not interpret monastic usages in a human way. They considered that fidelity required putting into practice the same observances that the earlier generations had devised. Thus there was only one way to be a fervent monk or nun: the way things were done when you entered.

Without a culture in depth a person is limited by the closed horizons within which he or she was formed. It requires a rather detailed and full grasp of history and of the philosophy of history as well to develop a sense of the relative, time-conditioned nature of social and cultural practices. Only someone who knows the Tradition in considerable breadth of detail that allows for a grasp of the suppleness with which the more gifted and holy abbots had expressed its values can rightly judge the validity and usefulness of specific ways of embodying the values of that

65. Ibid., 94.
66. Ibid., 119.

tradition. In our Order, for example, this question has comes up repeatedly in connection with the reform of de Rancé. It requires a sound understanding of our heritage to do justice to his contribution to reform in his time, and realistically to appreciate his virtues and limits for people today. Merton commented on this with some strong feelings, having discovered how frustrating it was to attempt to influence such a situation.

> One is left with a feeling that the house is full of people who have no notion what it is all about, and this is because they cannot accept the dead, but zealous voluntarism of the people who make it all consist in keeping rules, period: and not accepting this they have nothing better. . . . That reminds me: are they doing anything about de Rancé this year? He is the granddaddy of the will power boys and yet there was a lot that was really genuine and admirable in his reform. But once again people refuse to take a really sane perspective on such things: it has got to be all or nothing. Either Rancé is the greatest saint of the Order or nothing. Nothing in between. We cannot accept the fact that a man can be a serious, good, in some ways admirable monk, and at the same time an obsessive neurotic, defeating himself and blocking the Holy Ghost by his own best zeal. Yet that is the kind of thing we have most of in our Order.[67]

As often happened Fr. Louis tended to overstate his case, to enhance the contrast between opposing views. True to form, however, indeed, some paragraphs later in the same letter, he has kinder things to say about the people in the Order. He refers to the unity of charity that is so obvious and that calls for deep gratitude, and ends by observing that "the monastic life is a great thing and there is much life in it yet, many possibilities of growth." This is another instance of how easy it is to take statements of Merton's out of their larger context and prove either side of an argument.

A series of recent studies published in the United States by two psychologists, one at Cornell University, not far from my monastery of the Genesee, analyzes a problem that constitutes probably the chief difficulty confronting anyone who sets out to

67. Ibid., 174.

reform and renew any sizeable institution, or even to correct an individual whose performance is inadequate and unacceptable. Since it throws light on the situation that Fr. Louis confronted over a period of twenty years or so, it seems worthwhile to report their conclusion: the paradoxical truth that **incompetence often accompanies overconfidence.** Upon reflection this finding has more reasonableness to it than first appears. Persons who did poorest when asked to evaluate their level of skill in tests of logic, grammar, and humor "grossly overestimated" their success. Those who performed well tended to underestimate their ability.

Common sense would seem to dictate that confidence would be proportional to competence and that the less effective would have a proportionately lower level of trust in their performance, and that the more competent would have a measure of confidence that parallels their efficiency. But common sense reasoning often overlooks some significant element operative in real life. The significant insight in this study is that it requires the same kind of knowledge to evaluate one's performance as to perform the given task. In other words, only those who know, know what they know; those who do not know commonly do not know they are ignorant!

Another interesting and pertinent observation was that, when asked to compare their performance with their peers, those who were incompetent became more sure of themselves, whereas the competent, who examined the replies of their peers, improved their self-confidence. Only after further training did the incompetent display a more realistic self-evaluation. The researchers final word after a further study of the competence of drivers is that overconfidence is a widespread human trait.[68]

To apply this finding to our present consideration we might paraphrase these observations with the following: ignorance of the tradition is generally accompanied by an unrealistic confidence in one's way of thinking and living its values. Within certain limits this principle operates in the spiritual life in general as the great spiritual masters such as Saints Basil, Augustine, and Bernard realized. Only those who know God know how

68. Reported in the *New York Times, Review of the Week* (January 23, 2000) 2.

little they know; those who know little readily overestimate the measure of their knowledge and are more content to accept what they know as adequate to their needs.

Those who know most are the most eager to increase their knowledge and the more apt to underestimate how much they already do understand. There have been periods in the history of our Order when, as a result of broad cultural shifts and other social changes, the superiors and monks of the Order, in spite of their zeal and faith, had not adequately assimilated the spirit and values of the Founders and of the second generation of Cistercians who had contributed so much to the integrated spirituality that was at once so favorable to humanism and to divinization.

In God's providence Fr. Louis entered the Order just as the whole Church was coming to the end of the four hundred-year epoch dominated by the spirit and theology of the Council of Trent. Our Order was strongly marked by that same spirit and practices to a point where major features of the Cistercian charism were obscured if not altogether buried. Merton felt the need long before most others to remedy this situation. His efforts along these lines, though unrecognized for what they were at the time, were part of a movement in the Church as a whole, and especially in France, that led to Vatican II and an extensive reform that sought to respond to the signs of the times. His perceptiveness, his courageous persistence, and his loyal fidelity in spite of misunderstandings and frustrations, places Merton among the prophetic voices that called the Order to follow in the footsteps of the holy Fathers, and the Church to return to the wholeness of the Gospel.

IV. RENEWAL AND WORDS

> Thus words have no essential meaning.
> They are means of locomotion
> From backward to forward
> Along an infinite horizontal plane,
> Created by the history which they themselves destroy.
> They are the makers of our only reality
> The backward-forward working of the web
> The movement into the web.
>

The Tower of Babel[69]

History shows us that renewal of the Cistercian charism is a task set for each generation of monks. Father Louis had a particularly acute sense of the need for his generation's restoration of the more profound values of the monastic life as it had been lived in our Order for some centuries. In particular, he experienced the style of monastic life in his own monastery as unsuited for the current needs of American men who had entered the cloister in order to seek God. Gethsemani's monastic style, he believed, did not allow sufficient flexibility for individuals to work out personal encounters with and then personal appropriation of the profound values of Cistercian monasticism. He saw the need for revision of observances to be sure, but clearly more than that was requisite for an efficacious formation to a life of union with God that effected a real transformation of the monk. "What is needed," he wrote, "is not only new rules but new structures and new life. What is also needed is a new outlook and a

---

69. *The Collected Poems of Thomas Merton*, 21.

new faith in the capacities of modern men to be monks in a new way."[70]

Father Jean Leclercq noted that earlier than others Merton foresaw that the centuries old centralizing approach to observances and, within limits, structures of the Order was no longer feasible. Having a single set of detailed usages for monasteries in very different cultures and for communities living in widely divergent circumstances of weather, economy, and education could no longer allow for adequate response to the specific requirements of the individual persons called to the Cistercian life. What needed stressing was the monk's personal union with God and those expressions of vitality in each age that were called already by our Lord "the signs of the times." True renewal had to keep that end in mind above all other considerations and create a manner of supporting and stimulating those characteristics which favor attaining to this goal of union with God. With this aim in mind he made the following observations.

> Authentic renewal is going to demand a great deal of variety and originality in experimentation. Obviously, the mere issuing of decrees and ordinances from the top down, carried out mechanically on a massive scale, will simply stifle what life is left in monasticism. . . The true strength of monasticism is to be sought in its capacity for renunciation, silence, prayer, faith and its realization of the cross in our life.[71]

It was not too long after Merton died that the General Chapter elaborated and gave legal force to the Statute on Unity and Pluralism, which legislated the right of each community to establish its own usages within the framework of norms common to the Order. As this process takes place, the words that serve to name the various aspirations, practices, and values that constitute the tradition must themselves undergo a rebirth so as to take on new life. Passing on the tradition then entails the renewal of the words that make up the essential and monastic vocabulary as

---

70. Thomas Merton, *Contemplation in a World of Action* (Garden City, NY: Doubleday & Co., 1971) 11.
71. Ibid., 9.

understood in the Cistercian tradition. Words, after all, are symbols of realities, whether objects, experiences, ideas, or images. As the experience of these realities wears thin and even disappears, words lose content, are devoid of spirit, and fall flat upon the ears. To serve their full purpose they must be revitalized so as to connect with the personal inner world of the hearer or the one who reads them.

The same words obviously have a general sense that is commonly accepted by those who speak the language of which words are elements, but fully to perform their function, words must also have affective, emotional, and imaginative associations. To live, words must awaken interest, desire, curiosity, stimulate determination. Once they cease to speak with such force they become hollow, they wither, and die. People are united to form community only when they share such words as move their hearts and imagination.

Each of us has his own personal thesaurus made up of words that have specific associations of these kinds for us. C. G. Jung came to understand this truth rather early on in his career and devised a simple psychological test based on it. He drew up a list of 100 words and presented it to the subject to be tested. He asked the subject to say, without any censoring, the first word that comes to mind upon hearing the test word read out and timed the responses for each word. The word "mother" for example might evoke the reply "loving" in one case and, in another instance, "threatening." That answer might come rapidly or with considerable delay due to feelings of guilt, anxiety, and the like. From the answers given to the whole list one can get a fairly broad idea of the particular affective traits of the one tested. This feature of our human psyche has a very large application to the spiritual life of each person. Words play a much larger role in our lives than we are inclined to advert to. Words can be life saving, they can cause joy, or bring about deep depression that is life threatening. They can be a source of attraction to some person or some way of life or destroy the respect one had for a given individual or some field of endeavor.

Take the word "monk." It is laden with affect for some and readily evokes images of one kind or another for a large number of persons who come across it. Put it together with "Trappist" or "Cistercian" and that image will be modified in some way. Certainly for many thousands of people all over the world who have read Merton, their reaction to the term "Trappist monk" or "Cistercian monk" is much different now than it was before they were exposed to his writings. That is the case for many monks as well as for laypersons. For many Fr. Louis created a new image of what a monk is, what kind of person it is who becomes a monk, how monastic life affects those who enter upon it over the years. Is a monk someone who cannot compete or make his way in society, a withdrawn personality? Is he someone who has no interest in life on earth, a person who cannot relate healthily to society, to people, especially to women, who has no concept of politics?

As I myself discovered when I studied in a psychiatry department of a university hospital and clinic, and in later dealings with psychiatrists and others, even sophisticated persons held such distorted views of monks. Most, however, simply viewed monks as unknown and mysterious men who were inaccessible and of no particular interest since they were not met with in real life.

A reading of the *Spiritual Directory* of 1928 in its English version readily explains why a modern, healthy person would be likely to form an unfavorable image of anyone who lived as a Trappist. There is nothing that would connect with the imagination and appeal to the ideals of the youth that would enable them to identify with the formation offered. The *Spiritual Directory* would have conveyed to an American that a monk is expected to conform to a system that would control every aspect of the monk's life. This over-controlled environment was a caricature of the Cistercian way as depicted by St. Bernard. Merton himself has described his impressions upon opening this book, given him by the guest-master, the day after he arrived at Gethsemani. He felt the need to get some further light on the life lived in the community just before he entered the cloister to become a postulant.

> I went back to my room and started puzzling my head over the copy of the *Spiritual Directory*. . . It is easy enough to say,

"Trappists are called to lead lives of prayer and penance," because after all there is a sense in which everybody is called to lead that kind of a life. It is also easy enough to say that Cistercians are called to devote themselves entirely to contemplation. . . . then the question arises: "What do you mean by contemplation anyway?" From the Spiritual Directory I learned that "the Holy Mass, the Divine Office, Prayer and pious reading, which form the exercises of the contemplative life, occupy the major part of our day." It was a frigid and unsatisfying sentence. The phrase "pious reading" was a gloomy one, and somehow the thought that the contemplative life was something that was divided into "exercises" was of a sort that would normally have depressed me.[72]

Merton's comment on the experience well describes my own reaction to this work when I was a young monk: ". . . it is one of the tiresome minor details of all religious life today, that one must receive a large proportion of spiritual nourishment dished up in the unseasoned jargon of transliterated French."[73] Later Merton found that the French version was less off-putting, but still the impression this passage gave was hardly calculated to present the figure of a monk as a fulfilled, mature human person. Nor does it serve to inspire a love of contemplative prayer.

Today in my monastery of the Genesee we give the men who enter the community Merton's book *The Monastic Journey*.[74] It speaks a language and depicts a goal they readily identify with. It is not only the style, however, that makes the work palatable; the content, his way of describing the same practices that the Directory had treated renders the message accessible and the effort to attain to the values spoken of appear eminently worthwhile. Indirectly it presents the figure of a monk as a person formed in the modern world, capable of entering into a wholesome process of spiritual transformation through a faith-filled participation in our Cistercian life. The expectation is that this formation will enable him to employ his gifts of nature and grace in such a way as to make a worthy contribution to his own com-

72. *The Seven Storey Mountain*, 374.
73. Ibid.
74. *The Monastic Journey*, edited by Brother Patrick Hart, OCSO (Kansas City: Sheed Andrews and McMeel, Inc. 1977).

munity and through the community to the Church and society through seeking God.

It not too much to say that the whole of Thomas Merton's written *oeuvre* contributes to forming a more realistic and worthy concept of who and what a monk is and that he, more than any other person in our times, and perhaps since the twelfth century, managed to create in a large public a fresh concept of the monk as a person.

Merton defines a monk in terms that give a more concrete image of what it means to dedicate oneself to the search for God in all truth. His concept of monk cannot properly be appreciated without exploring a number of closely associated terms and the realities to which they point. The characteristic word field in which he sets forth his thought about renewal in our Order, and, increasingly, in the Church as a whole, included such terms as *the true self* and its various paraphrases and synonyms, *personal identity, contemplation, transformation, divinization,* and *humanism.* We can approach the study of his teaching by a consideration of any one of these words for each will lead us to the same ultimate truth; each represents an element that takes its meaning from the same central reality, namely, the mystery of life in the glorified Christ.

Moreover, each of these terms has reference to a facet of the tradition that is present already in the most representative figures of our Cistercian and Patristic heritage, as Merton himself made abundantly evident. *Humanism, true self,* and *identity* are modern terms used by Merton in such a way as to demonstrate how they are legitimate, updated expressions that elaborate insights found in these earlier authors. He understood his role to be not that of an original thinker but rather that of a modern representative of the best monastic and Cistercian traditions. He was able to articulate the essential and permanent values of our tradition because he experienced them deeply himself in his search for God. He reflected on these values in light of the contributions of authors whose writings largely determined the character of modern consciousness as such, who have set the dominant tone of the Western culture in which all of us have been formed.

Let us examine the word *contemplation*. This is one of the most fundamental terms in the monastic vocabulary that has become common currency in modern times. It is often used to define the monastic life and to distinguish it from other forms of religious life. In conformity with Canon Law, for instance, our Constitutions define our Order as *a monastic institute integrally ordered to contemplation* (CST 2). Accordingly, how the word *contemplation* is presented colors the concept one forms of a monastery and the image of a monk.

But contemplation is a difficult concept to define. No attempt has managed to prove adequate since, like the word *mysticism* with which it is closely associated, it is one of the least susceptible of being defined to the satisfaction of any broad public. A definition that satisfies philologists and patristic scholars may prove unacceptable to theologians. If contemplation is to speak effectively to people of our time, it must be provided with a content that makes of it an exciting term, one that stimulates people to pursue a life of deeper prayer. Contemplation requires associations that lend it life and color.

That such a refurbishing of this word was badly needed by the Order is made abundantly evident from the way it was dealt with in the *Spiritual Directory* given to Merton and used by Novices Masters until the early '60s, when Fr. Louis and others, such as Fr. Placide Deseilles of Bellefontaine, had offered alternatives. The *Directory*, Merton wrote, stated some cautious words about infused contemplation, adding that it is not necessary but God sometimes "vouchsafed" it. Though it encourages monks to live as to be disposed for mystical graces, yet Merton's reaction to this presentation was that a monk should be very cautious about manifesting any serious interest in higher prayer.

Some years after he was in the monastery, just before the publication of his autobiography, Fr. Louis wrote a letter to Fr. Raymond Flanagan, a well known author and monk of Gethsemani, in which he sets down his view of the need for some serious changes in the Order in view of a renewal favoring the formation of contemplatives. He lists a number of suggested changes that he considered essential in addition to describing the obstacles to the cultivation of contemplative prayer. The whole of this document deserves to be read both for the light it casts on the concrete situation at Gethsemani at the time as well as for revealing Merton's keen awareness of the need for change and his specific remedies.[75]

In his letter to Fr. Raymond Merton points out some striking historical facts from our tradition. For example, he notes that nothing in the early Cistercian documents speaks of contemplation. The word does not occur. What they sought, he adds, was the genuine, simple cenobitic monastic life lived with fervor. In the vocabulary of Evagrius Pontus, and then of John Cassian who was his disciple, this is the *active* life. It was St. Bernard who introduced into the Order a school of mysticism that resulted in some houses of the Order actually living a life of contemplative prayer. However, there grew up the tendency to get too involved in business, to add penances and multiply observances and thus to be over busy. Interior prayer of the heart and contemplation proper were neglected and often even unknown. These problems, Merton affirms, remained in his own time and monastery. One reason is that a number of monks neither understood what contemplation is or how to use leisure when they had it.

In a subsequent communication to Fr. Raymond, Fr. Louis analyzes the spirituality of various contemplative Orders and concludes that there is no great difference among them; those variations in observances that exist he considered minor.[76]

> The goal in all cases is prayer based on the Presence of God, and kept as simple as possible, constant return to God's presence, use of ejaculations according to individual appeal and not much stress on discursive meditation. . . . The other ancillary problems are also the same: how to keep united with Superiors. . . what to do when you are tired and fed up.

Following up on these observations Merton wrote repeatedly on issues related to the purpose of monastic life and contemplative prayer in particular. In *The Monastic Journey* there

---

75. Thomas Merton, *Witness to Freedom*, edited by William H. Shannon (Farrar, Straus & Giroux, 1994) 233ff.
76. Ibid., 235.

are a number of fine texts on contemplation through which Merton leads the reader to want to enter upon the way that leads to it, while showing how it relates to the rest of the spiritual life, above all to the person of Christ. For example in the chapter "Basic Principles of Monastic Spirituality" (originally published in 1957) he relates contemplation intimately to the monastic vocation, to the Church at large, and to the mystery of Christ.

There can be no doubt that the monastic vocation is one of the most beautiful in the Church of God. The "contemplative life," as the life of the monastic orders is usually called, is a life entirely devoted to the mystery of Christ, to living the life of God who gives Himself to us in Christ. It is a life totally abandoned to the Holy Spirit, a life of humility, obedience, solitude, silence, prayer, in which we renounce our own desires and our own ways in order to live in the liberty of the sons of God, guided by the Holy Spirit speaking through our superiors, our Rule, and in the inspirations of His grace within our hearts.[77]

The rest of this article associates a detailed description of monastic life with the concept of contemplative prayer. To be a monk is to be an intimate with God at least in the desire of the heart, and to be on the way to intimacy with God is already to be heading for a form of contemplation.

Merton suggests what Karl Rahner later made explicit in his writings on mysticism in everyday life. The German theologian showed how the mystical experience and the knowledge of God attendant upon it is arrived at by various practices in addition to the special kind of perception and activity covered by the word *contemplation*. In these ordinary events the individual himself may well not recognize the more direct contact with God mediated in the acts of daily life, and yet in fact be involved with a profound and immediate communication from God. Merton's way of situating contemplative life in the whole context of monastic living hints at the same important insight. Not all mystics in a monastic community are contemplative, endowed with special graces of supernatural prayer. Perhaps a majority of truly mystical graces are unrecognized as such because they are masked by the ordinariness of the occasions that mediate them.

77. Ibid., 11.

There are many other passages where Fr. Louis treats of contemplation. Often, without treating of the term formally, the reality of contemplation is everywhere, forming the background of his discussion of what it means to live in a Cistercian monastery as a monk. His chapter called "Monastic Peace" reveals a contemplative atmosphere in which the whole of his subject is bathed. The general effect of these pages is to elevate the concept of what it is to be a monk by linking it closely to life in God and to contemplative knowledge in Christ. In this manner the concept of monk and the associations of the word contemplation are both enriched and renewed (cf. p. 46ff.).

In treating of contemplation, Merton sought to develop a context and a language that related it to the rest of monastic life and enhanced its content by anchoring it in the mystery of the Risen Christ. In addition, he examined its various facets in detail and showed how it was understood and put into practice by various saintly mystics in the past. Above all, he studied Cassian's teaching on this theme in considerable detail. Since, as Merton states, Cassian is probably the most influential writer in Western monasticism, his doctrine is at the heart of our Cistercian tradition.

Merton had studied Cassian carefully and admired him greatly and made him a prominent figure in his teaching to the juniors and novices. To understand his views on Cassian's doctrine on contemplation is to understand a major source of the Merton's theology of contemplative prayer.

One of the less known and important nuances of this doctrine that Merton, alone of Cassian's interpreters as far as I am aware, appreciated and stressed is the fact that contemplation of God on earth has two forms (Conference. 1:15). This nuance may well be a refinement not intended by the fifth century author and an instance of Merton's fruitful *eisegesis*, amounting to a gloss by Cassian's twentieth-century translator and commentator. The Latin of the original reads as follows:

> Sunt autem aliae quoque huiusmodi innumerae contemplationes, quae pro qualitate vitae ac puritate cordis in nostris sensibus oriuntur, quibus deus vel videtur mundis obtutibus vel tenetur (*Collationes* I.15 S.C. 42, 97).

In his chapter called "The Humanity of Christ in Monastic Prayer" Merton translates the phrase as presenting two distinct ways of knowing God. He interprets this to say: "God is seen with pure vision or else is possessed" (i.e., by love).[78] The French translator, on the other hand, has an interpretation that does not discern any such distinction. He rather understands, probably correctly (though with a considerable lessening of theological interest), the *vel* of Cassian to be equivalent to *et*, and the second verb as functionally synonymous with *videtur*. ". . . *c'est Dieu qui est vu et possédé en de pures intuitions* [it is God who is seen and possessed with pure intuitions]."

For Merton, then, if not for Cassian, there are two mystical modes: one consists in seeing God through his creation, the other is to possess him by love. This is much more significant as an insight than first appears, having important practical significance for all those seeking to live a life of prayer but who have no special gifts for what is classically described as infused contemplation. This doctrine was later to serve as the basis for teaching that came to be known as the mysticism of everyday life.

Other features of this body of doctrine are more widely recognized today, but at the time were the possession largely of scholars. Cassian's teaching on *theologia* and *theoria physike* was certainly not known by the large majority of monks who at that period read very little of the Fathers of the Church. Nor were other religious and Christian laymen familiar with such texts. Merton eagerly pursued his attraction for Cassian and other Fathers; his interest in their writings proved lifelong. He began to teach them in the early 1950s and contributed appreciably to spreading their teachings within the Order and to others as well.

In *The Ascent to Truth*, one of his earlier books, he contributed to disseminating among monks of the Order and many laypersons as well the spirituality of the more important mystical writers of the Church. Other more academic and scholarly authors, especially in France and England, had done more basic and original research. They published their findings in a style more suited to theologians and specialists than to most monks. The

78. Ibid., 91.

older members of the Order were not attracted to the scientific analysis of mystical and contemplative writings and the young had not as yet received adequate exposure or training to profit from the fine scholarship that came out of France and Germany especially. Merton, who followed these studies assiduously, made use of their results in his classes and presented them in *The Ascent to Truth* with a clarity of expression that a good number of readers found appealing. He himself grew very dissatisfied with this work precisely because it was written in a more didactic style than altogether suited to his particular gifts. However, he filtered the data he had gleaned from other authors through his own experiences of prayer so that the general impression is that this work is a personal presentation of the mystical theologians who have contributed most to the understanding of contemplation and mystical experience in general.

The following, for instance, is a sample of how he could make it seem natural for a modern reader to cultivate an interest in the writings of the ancients that deal with the more profound kinds of prayer.

> We imprison ourselves in falsity by our love for the feeble, flickering light of illusion and desire. We cannot find the true light unless this false light be darkened. We cannot find true happiness unless we deprive ourselves of the *ersatz* happiness of empty diversion. Peace, true peace, is only to be found through suffering and we must seek light in darkness.
>
> There are, in Christian tradition, a theology of light and a theology of darkness. On these two lines travel two mystical trends. There are the great theologians of light: Origen, Saint Augustine, Saint Bernard, Saint Thomas Aquinas. And there are the great theologians of darkness: Saint Gregory of Nyssa, Pseudo-Dionysius, Saint John of the Cross. The two lines travel side by side. [79]

It is typical of Merton that he follows this summary of the schools of Christian mysticism with a reference to Zen Buddhism that points up the distinction between the two approaches to illusion

---

79. Thomas Merton, *The Ascent to Truth* (New York: Harcourt, Brace and Company, 1951) 25.

while indicating that there are also areas of common agreement. His interest in Eastern religions anticipated by a decade the popular movements that in the sixties spread through Europe and the Americas.

> There are pages in the works of Saint Gregory of Nyssa—as there are also in Saint John of the Cross—which might easily fit into a context of Zen Buddhism of Patanjali's yoga. But we must remember that, when a Christian mystic speaks of the created world as an illusion and as "nothingness," he is only using a figure of speech. The words are not to be taken literally and they are not ontological. The world is metaphysically real. Creatures can lead us efficaciously to the knowledge and love of their Creator and ours.[80]

Merton held the view that contemplation of itself opened up the individual to the universal, the whole of creation and of mankind; it is Catholic in its scope, including all that is within its embracing vision when it is sufficiently pure. Accordingly, he was persuaded that preparation for the contemplative life would best be furthered when it included an intelligent familiarity with Eastern thought and practices.

In an article he wrote entitled "Christian Culture Needs Oriental Wisdom" Merton describes the qualities of Eastern thought that, when cultivated, facilitate a contemplative lifestyle and can prepare the heart for responding to the graces of mystical prayer. His interpretation of certain classical works of Confucian provenance is a convincing argument for including some such studies in the monastic formation program. For example, he is able to show, contrary to certain other interpreters, how filial piety, so central to this tradition is, in its original tendency, not rigid formalism but is rather personalistic.

> . . . filial piety is not simply a cult of the parent as such, but a development of one's own gifts in honor of the parents who gave them to us. Then, when we reach manhood and our parents are old, we make a fitting return to them

---

80. Ibid., 26.

by loving support. This basic attitude is said to be "the foundation of virtue and the root of civilization."[81]

He further points out that Christian religion is complete of itself, being revealed by God and having all the essentials required for salvation; it certainly is not deficient so as to stand in need of non-Christian doctrines. However, in order to be more fully incarnate in cultures and in the persons who are formed by the various cultures, the Christian religion can profit greatly from selectively utilizing the insights and practices of these religions. This was done in regard to Jewish religion, Greek philosophy and Roman law.

In this short essay it becomes evident that Merton had an remarkable capacity for entering into thought systems that are foreign to his own tradition with a view to understanding them so as to profit from what is valid in their teachings, not only for himself but for others, and especially for contemplatives, who seek a fuller, deeper life. He does not seek to refute but to comprehend with sympathy. His approach is not primarily analytical, logical analysis but sympathetic reception in view of assimilating what is useful for fuller comprehension of the Christian mystery.

> The values hidden in Oriental thought actually reveal themselves only on the plane of spiritual experience, or perhaps, if you like, of aesthetic experience. They belong, of course, to the natural order; but they certainly have deep affinities with supernatural wisdom itself. [82]

In the last decade of his life, as he continued to develop his views on contemplative prayer, Merton was to devote a considerable portion of his time to exploring Oriental wisdom. Zen Buddhism in particular held a great attraction for him as it inculcates a kind of experience that represents a human reflection of the nothingness which, in Merton's prayer, was the condition of man before God. (Later on the Dalai Lama would pay tribute

---

81. Thomas Merton, *A Thomas Merton Reader*, edited by Thomas P. McDonnell (New York: Harcourt, Brace & World, Inc.) 323.
82. Ibid., 326.

to his profound understanding of Buddhist experience, calling him the equivalent of a Doctor of Mysticism.)

Merton makes his position on Zen quite clear. He is interested in it not as a system of thought or as a religion, but rather as a pointer to a transcendent experience of the void. Zen consciousness as such does not judge and classify what it perceives with any finality. "If it seems to judge and distinguish, it does so only enough to point beyond judgment to the pure void."[83] *(Zen and the Birds of Appetite, 6)*. He was interested in pursuing this wisdom as a help to attain "to the freedom of the sons of God." Merton follows Meister Eckhart's teaching here that nothing must remain in man's consciousness if God is to act upon him with perfect freedom. For "God himself must be the place in which He acts."[84] Toward the end of his life Merton increasingly emphasized this negative aspect of contemplation out of a heightened consciousness of the transcendent and infinite God. His involvement with Zen was only but deeply a function of his attaining a fuller grasp of the God of Jesus Christ.

---

83. Thomas Merton, *Zen and the Birds of Appetite* (New York: New Directions Press, 1968) 6.
84. Ibid., 9.

V. THE ROLE OF CONTEMPLATION IN CISTERCIAN RENEWAL

Merton's exploration of Eastern religious traditions influenced the evolutions of his views on contemplation. There have been widely differing opinions expressed as to how large or small an influence such interests exerted upon his views concerning monastic life in general and even his faith. A careful examination of his extensive writings on this subject reveals that there is no basis for the opinion that Merton's faith in the Church or in his Cistercian vocation was ever modified, much less weakened, by his interest in the East. His contacts with these traditions both by study and dialogue with members of these traditions certainly had an impact on his views of monastic life and contemplation. This influence was a wholesome one in that it led him to emphasize the fundamental simplicity and other central elements of the contemplative life.

Even before he entered the monastery, and indeed prior to his entering the Catholic Church, he encountered the Eastern spiritual world in the person of Bramachari, a Hindu monk who had come to the United States on a visit. In the pages of his autobiography, as he tells the story of their meeting and subsequent friendship, the warm gratitude and affection that he felt toward this man shines through the account. It was 1938 when the two of them first met and Merton was favorably impressed by his striking simplicity and directness of manner.[85]

Something of the openness to the monks of the East that was to be so prominent a feature of the later Merton appears here already in the spontaneous respect and trust that marked

---

85. Cf. *The Seven Storey Mountain*, 195.

their relations from the first. He wrote, "I became very fond of Bramachari, and he of me. We got along very well together, especially since he sensed that I was trying to feel my way into a settled religious conviction, and into some kind of a life that was centered, as his was, on God." The two men showed a mutual respect for one another's beliefs. Merton noted that the Hindu avoided any attempt to gain influence over him, while Merton's own demeanor invited frank and open exchanges. This trait that seems to have grown naturally out of Merton's earlier formation was to prove a great asset when he became involved in ecumenical encounters. It was surely a major reason why Merton was so readily taken into the confidence of some of the best representatives of Eastern traditions as D. T. Suzuki and the Dalai Lama.

It was Bramachari who told the twenty-three-year-old student, still confused as to his orientation but beginning to seek a deeper spiritual life, that he should read St. Augustine's *Confessions* and *The Imitation of Christ*. "Yes, you must read those books," the Hindu monk told him.

> It was not often that he spoke with this kind of emphasis. . . . After all, it is rather ironical that I had turned spontaneously to the east in reading about mysticism, . . . So now I was told that I ought to turn to the Christian tradition, to St. Augustine—and told by a Hindu monk [86]

But Fr. Louis's path to conversion had already oriented him to classical Catholic sources that he would have explored in any case. Being interested in art as an approach to life, he was profoundly influenced by Jacques Maritain's *Art and Scholasticism*. Eastern thought and practice had a certain influence on Merton's conversion and his interest in religious experience through his reading of the novelist Aldous Huxley. His book, *Ways and Means*, which treats of mysticism, helped the young Merton to belief in the reality of a supernatural order.

> Not only was there such a thing as a supernatural order, but as a matter of concrete experience, it was accessible, very close at hand, an extremely near, an immediate and

---

86. Ibid., 198.

most necessary source of moral vitality, and one which could be reached most simply, most readily by prayer, faith detachment, love. And the big conclusion from all this was: we must practice prayer and asceticism. Asceticism! The very thought of such a thing was a complete revolution in my mind.[87]

Ways and Means, heavily Buddhist inspired, thus influenced the association of contemplation in Merton's mind with ascetic practice and self-denial. Merton saw clearly the limits and shortcomings of this book by the time he wrote the tale of his conversion, but he never forgot his indebtedness to it, even after he left much of that eclectic work far behind.

Merton had early occupied himself with studying the Christian classics: Dante, St. Augustine, the *Summa* of St. Thomas, and St. John of the Cross, who was to become a favorite later, though he could not understand him well at this early period in his conversion. We hear no more about Eastern religions until some time well into his monastic years.

Once he entered Gethsemani, Merton continued his serious study of the Catholic Fathers and monastic classics, especially Cassian and later St. Bernard and other Cistercian Fathers. How sympathetically and attentively he read St. Augustine is evident from the informative and judicious introduction he wrote to the Everyman's edition of *The City of God*. Thus by the time he began seriously to read the Chinese Taoists and Japanese Zen classics he was solidly rooted in the Patristic and monastic spiritual traditions.

The appeal of these Asian thinkers for Merton was their emphasis on the fullness of meaning to be found in the concrete reality of ordinary life. This teaching he had already found to be implied in St. Benedict and the Desert Fathers. Increasingly, his own prayer, as we learn from his private journals, was an experience of *the void*. This experience of a radical emptiness is central to Zen. It helped him to understand the Chinese attitude of *Wu wei*, non-doing. Merton found in these writings a confirmation of the validity of his personal experience of God, and a confidence

87. Ibid., 185.

that came from a fuller understanding of its human as well as supernatural implications. His appreciation of contemplation as a form of knowledge accessible to all persons who seriously enter into their own heart was given firm support and extended in detail through his contact with such writers as Chuang Tzu on the great Tao and Daisetz Suzuki on Zen meditation and enlightenment.

Merton's book on Chuang Tzu reveals a remarkable firmness of treatment as to the meaning of this obscure poet who lived in the 4th and 3rd centuries B.C. In reading his analysis of the poems and the sureness with which he explains their subtle message, it becomes evident how great is the sympathy of thought and style that the twentieth century Trappist feels for this Chinese philosopher poet. Merton's own experience allows him to see what they have in common as well as what distinguishes their views of the deeper meaning of life. Centered as he is on life in Christ, Merton is keenly aware of the limits of the Taoist vision, but he is more conscious of what unites the Christian with the natural philosopher. Merton comments, for example, on what bearing Chuang Tzu's work might have on St. Paul's teaching about grace. He sees connections most would fail to observe in the comparison.

> Chuang Tzu. . . sees that mere virtuousness is without meaning and without deep effect either in the life of the individual or in society.
>
> Once this is clear, one can reasonably see a certain analogy between Chuang Tzu and St. Paul. The analogy must certainly not be pushed too far. Chuang Tzu lacks the profoundly theological mysticism of St. Paul. But his teaching about the spiritual liberty of *wu wei* and the relation of virtue to the indwelling Tao is analogous to Paul's teaching on faith and grace, contrasted with "the works of the Old Law." The relation of the Chuang Tzu book to the *Analects* of Confucius is not unlike that of the Epistles to the Galatians and Romans to the Torah.[88]

Merton's elucidation of both the Tao and Zen experiences contribute to anchoring his own personal contemplative experience of God in a human context much wider than Cistercian

---

88. Thomas Merton, *The Way of Chuang Tzu* (New York: New Directions Press, 1965) 24–25.

monasticism; wider even than the Christian tradition. These connections serve to enhance the validity and worth of Cistercian tradition. They reveal very specific ways in which the contemplative knowledge of God in Christ completes the limited but profound insights into the workings of the human spirit in its interaction with history, society, and all that constitutes human life. Merton demonstrates how the transcendent experience of the Catholic mystic at one level is analogous to certain qualities and insights of the Taoist natural philosopher. He thus gives fresh luster to the word *contemplation* and conveys with a more forcible vitality what perspectives open up to the person who seriously pursues a contemplative way of life.

At the same time, Merton became increasingly sensitive to the ways in which theology and metaphysical presuppositions impinge upon spiritual experience and mystical insights in particular. In his extensive Introduction to Dr. John Wu's book *The Golden Age of Zen* (1967) he carefully elaborated in extensive detail certain of the manifold questions associated with this issue. He so treats the subject that he enables the reader to become aware of a variety of implications of the contemplative experience that most of us had not adverted to before. In this way he further advances his presentation of what is involved when one speaks of contemplation. These pages represent his most refined and detailed treatment of the nature of Zen experience of the void and what experience might be comparable in Christian mystical experience. Merton's entire discussion bears study. Here is a sampling of his presentation.

> We keep returning to one central question in two forms: the relation of objective doctrine to subjective mystic (or metaphysical) experience, and the difference between this relationship in Christianity and in Zen. In Christianity the objective doctrine retains priority both in time and in eminence. In Zen the experience is always prior, not in time but in importance. This is because Christianity is based on supernatural revelation and Zen, discarding all idea of any revelation and even taking a very independent view of sacred tradition (at least written), seeks to penetrate the natural ontological ground of being.[89]

89. Thomas Merton, *Zen and the Birds of Appetite* (New York: New Directions Press, 1968) 45.

After Merton's death a number of those who wrote about his life and work spoke as if he had become more of a Buddhist than Christian. How far that misses the mark becomes evident in the course of this closely reasoned essay written not long before he died. He was keenly aware of how the mystery of Christ is central to the contemplative experience of the Cistercian.

> [W]e must not neglect the great importance of experience in Christianity. But Christian experience always has a special modality, due to the fact that it is inseparable from the mystery of Christ and the collective life of the Church, the Body of Christ. To experience the mystery of Christ mystically or otherwise is always to transcend the merely individual psychological level and to "experience with the Church *(sentire cum ecclesia)*."[90]

An additional point that Merton stresses in this treatment of Zen is its emphatic insistence on direct experience. In some way this is the whole content of Zen and he is adept at enabling the reader to grasp with great insight just what is entailed by this practical focus. He then is at pains to emphasize that

> Zen explains nothing. It just sees. Sees what? Not an Absolute object but Absolute Seeing.
> Though this may seem very remote from Christianity, which is definitely a message, we must nevertheless remember the importance of *direct experience* in the Bible. All forms of "knowing" especially in the religious sphere, and especially where God is concerned, are valid in proportion as they are a matter of experience, and of intimate contact.[91]

As Merton develops these matters further, his treatment has the effect of enhancing our concept of what is entailed in the contemplative experience. His manner of presenting these insights has the effect of making contemplative life seem natural to human persons as such and so accessible to us today. In short, his study and meditation on Zen, as on the Tao, make significant contributions to his renewal of the term *contemplation* for our times.

90. Ibid., 46.
91. Ibid., 54.

Through Merton's studies of Zen and Taoism fresh significance also accrues to other practices and terms integral with our Cistercian heritage such as solitude, silence, and simplicity from this burnishing of the term *contemplation*. These elements which support and sustain a contemplative lifestyle derive their meaning from the higher goal which they serve and so share in the freshness associated with this purer experience of God resulting from *contemplation*.

While it is true that Thomas Merton's interest in Oriental religion grew and led to his writing a number of works dealing with Zen in particular, at the very end of his life Merton returned to the theme of contemplation and prayer in his own monastic tradition. Just before he left Gethsemani for the Bangkok meeting where he was to die, he completed what proved to be his final book. Most fittingly it was written with his attention on the monks of his own Cistercian Order especially. The title he gave it, used in the original edition, expressed well the context in which he treats of contemplation: *The Climate of Monastic Prayer*. Shortly after, in view of a wider audience, a second edition was published under the title: *Contemplative Prayer*.

As Douglas Steere observes in his Foreword, Merton chose to speak to the people of his age who stood in great need of contemplative prayer. He directed his words to "the small company of the expendable who have volunteered to give over their lives in abandonment to this 'Source of Life.'" If monks profited from his teaching to get free from the constrictions that inhibited their life of prayer, they in turn could act as ferment in society. Coming as it does at the very end of his life after his more serious study of Zen Buddhism, this work allows us to observe how Merton made use of his oriental studies. These final views on renewal in the Order witness to what he considered to be central to monastic life, the experience of God and that purity of heart that prepares us for union with him at the end.

For Merton never considered contemplation a worthier goal than that of life with God. Any number of writers, especially those influenced by Zen, can speak of meditation and contemplation and the associated concepts such as enlightenment, without reference to salvation or to God, much less to Christ. Merton was not among their number. He stated explicitly that if he had to choose between contemplation and eschatological realities, he would pick the latter every time. Already in 1953, in teaching us a course on the theology of St. Paul, he stressed emphatically how fundamental to the spiritual and monastic life is this orientation to the last things, above all the resurrection of the body. "If it were not for the resurrection of Christ, I would leave this monastery before Vespers," he exclaimed one day in class. Later on, in 1964, he recorded in his journal some further reflections on this topic, and at no point subsequently did he reverse himself, or even modify the primacy of his profound commitment to attain to union with the Risen Christ at the end.

> I am coming to see clearly the great importance of the concept of "realized eschatology"—the transformation of life and of human relations by Christ *now* rather than an eschatology focused on future cosmic events. . . . Realized eschatology is the heart of genuine Christian humanism and hence its tremendous importance for the Christian peace effort, for example.[92]

Thus prayer in its various forms and the experiences deriving from it are to be directed to this finality and derive their significance from the contribution they make to this ultimate goal. Contemplation is not an end in itself, nor merely an exercise that certain gifted persons find consoling and strengthening for the development of their personality, though these effects may well follow upon such prayer. In his Introduction to his work *The Climate of Monastic Prayer*, Merton's definition of a monk includes dedication to prayer. He writes: "The monk is a Christian who has responded to a special call from God, and has withdrawn from the more active concerns of a worldly life, in order to devote himself completely to repentance, 'conversion,' *metanoia*, renunciation and prayer. In positive terms, we must understand the monastic life above all as a life of prayer."[93]

---

92. Thomas Merton, *Dancing in the Water of Life*, The Journals Volume 5, edited by Robert E. Daggy (San Francisco: HarperSanFrancisco, 1997) 87.
93. Thomas Merton, *Contemplative Prayer* (New York: Image Books, 1969) 19.

While he writes especially for monks, he makes it clear that what he has to say about his subject is relevant to all Christian prayer though not necessarily applicable with the same measure of intensity of particular trials. Another point he makes is that he does not intend to treat of any techniques of prayer but rather its nature considered in itself. When he enters into his discussion of his subject it is significant that he refers not to any Zen authorities but to the Desert Fathers and Cassian. He retained his strong attachment to the Egyptian desert tradition right to the end.

In considering Merton's contribution to the Cistercian heritage in light of the signs of our modern times we find once again that his role was to disclose the relevance of its essential values for contemporary monks and Christians in general. Exposure to Oriental meditation and assimilation of much that he found pertinent in that tradition did not result in displacing the fundamental importance he gave to the same sources that had so much influenced St. Bernard, William of St. Thierry, and the early generation of Cistercians. In fact, his sensitive grasp of the insights of Zen masters into more intense and profound levels of spiritual experience would seem to have enhanced his conviction concerning the permanent validity of the doctrine of the Christian monks of the desert. He found in Zen an emphasis that was known to the Desert Fathers and Mothers: a notable simplicity and a concern to purify the mind from thoughts and images.

Another element that Merton sets out as distinctive of the Cistercian approach to prayer and of its abiding relevance for us today is the role of the Bible and especially the Psalms. The Psalter served the early Cistercians not only as a formulary for praise and petition but also as a source for a fuller understanding of the various movements and states of the heart in so far as they bear upon the spiritual life. They instinctively, for instance, interpreted references to war and struggle as referring to the interior warfare, the battle to purify and control the passions in the soul. The interrelatedness between self-knowledge in depth that facilitates the work of transformation of the affections on the one hand, and knowledge of God's holiness, his mercy and love on the other, is integral to progress in the life of prayer as these early monks conceived of it.

To recognize this interplay between knowledge of self, including the interior conflicts associated with the passions, and knowledge of God remains of radical importance for people of our time who in a complex society are subject to manifold and conflicting values and the images and passions linked to them. Naturally, the techniques and insights of modern psychology provide help unavailable in a simpler age. These can assist to make sense of the varied psychic movements and images that arise in the consciousness of those who learn to observe them and note their character.

As early as the fourth century Evagrius Ponticus, one of the Fathers of the Desert, had already urged this form of analytical meditation. His *Praktikos* has a number of chapters that reveal the results of his own practice of this form of self-analysis. For instance, here is one of a number of his descriptions. Note that he understands the demons to be the movers behind many of the passionate conflicts we experience; thus where he speaks of demons we can substitute passions that operate on a level accessible to demons.

> We must take care to recognize the different types of demons and take note of the circumstances of their coming. We shall know these from our thoughts (which we shall know from the objects). We ought to consider which of the demons are less frequent in their assaults, which are the more vexatious, which are the ones which yield the field more readily and which the more resistant. Finally, we should note which are the ones that make sudden raids and snatch off the spirit to blasphemy. Now it is essential to understand these matters so that when these various evil thoughts set their own proper forces to work we are in a position to address effective words against them, that is to say those words which correctly characterize the one present.[94]

Evagrius makes the crucial point here, the importance of which most persons fail to understand, that until we identify precisely the shades of our inner states, it is very difficult to modify our behavior directly, that is to say, by employing the appropriate remedy. Insight into the specific conflicts that di-

94. Evagrius Ponticus, *The Praktikos*, 43 (Kalamazoo, MI: Cistercian Studies series, 1970) 28.

vide us and bind up our energies and so hold us in bondage contributes to our psychological growth. Much more fruitful for this growth, however, are the fortunate and successful experiences that increase our sense of worth, with the result that indirectly they remove some of the emotional chains that bind our potential development. Merton, who was endowed with an uncommon spiritual and psychological perceptiveness, could appreciate this feature of desert spirituality and saw it as offering an abiding potential that persons of these times can tap into.

Thus Merton's teaching on prayer, including contemplation, is rooted in a traditional spirituality whose values he was able to recognize and point out as he commended their practices to his monastic readers. Another feature of desert spirituality that he emphasized was the prominence of the search for *quies, rest, tranquility of heart*. Attaining to this state served as a beacon that lighted the path of asceticism: ascetic practices are not to be cultivated for their own sake but in view of leading the monk to this *quies* in which God's communications could be received more directly. The *quies* was to be accompanied by a repetition of the word of God made with attention. This tranquility of spirit made the heart of the monk more susceptible to God's presence as he dwelt on the inspired words of Scripture that he took up as his prayer. Merton is able to find discreet references to contemplation in connection with those practices that lead to *quies*. When Arsenius is directed to go apart in silence *(tace, fuge, quiesce)*, what he receives is expressed in a less pretentious, simpler form than what we would refer to as a call to contemplation.

The spirituality of the Desert Fathers eschewed all pretentiousness and elitism; it stressed the ordinary. Merton found this feature of their lives and sayings particularly deserving of remark. It was a characteristic he himself had taken as a model and that he struggled to realize, as his journals make clear, in his own life over long periods.

The search to be one's true, ordinary self he felt was the Cistercian way, and yet his own life was so often filled with temptations to stand out, be singular, and recognized as special. One of the major attractions of Zen for him was its understanding that enlightenment results in a simplicity that frees a person from the desire to stand out from others, to be important in anyone's eyes, including one's own.

The early generations of monks did speak occasionally of "pure prayer," by which they meant obviously some elevated state that was the result of infused gifts. We find an instance of this experience and a detailed discussion of it in Cassian's tenth Conference. The word *mysticism*, however, was not yet coined. In fact, it is a relatively modern term, as Fr. Simon Tugwell insists. "Mysticism," he writes, "is notoriously a slippery word and it is also, of course, a modern word whose application in historical investigation is not straightforward."[95] Just how modern appears from the fact that the first instance of the word *mysticism* in English dates only from 1736; the French term *mysticisme* occurs about seventy years later in *1804*, so that Merton is quite correct to focus on the term *quies* (ἡσυχία in the original Greek text) rather than use the more modern terminology. In the Orthodox world a whole school of spirituality evolved around this concept and came to be known as Hesychasm.

Merton's treatment of *quies* then serves to relate Cistercian spirituality, which adopted the desert teaching on "quiet" as integral to the monastic ideal, to Hesychasm. In this way he indicates how contemplative prayer in the Cistercian tradition has a great deal in common with this venerable Eastern way which itself has undergone a renewal in the second half of the twentieth century.[96]

In 1959 Merton undertook an extensive revision of his thinking on contemplation as set out in *What Is Contemplation?* The manuscript of this work underwent four editions and remained incomplete at his death. However, he stated clearly he felt it should be published someday. The complicated history of this work has been well worked out by William H. Shannon who rightly recognizes its merits. In fact, after his death it was published as a series of eight separate chapters under the title *The Inner Experience*. Fr. Louis explains the reason for this reworking of a topic he had treated earlier in a letter to a friend. Speaking of his earlier treatment he wrote

---

95. Simon Tugwell, Review of Bernard McGinn's *The Foundations of Mysticism* in *The Journal of Theological Studies* 44 (1993) 685.
96. *The Wisdom of the Desert*, 20.

It is all very unsatisfactory to me. In fact a lot of it disgusts me. I was much too superficial and too cerebral at the time. I seem to have ignored the wholeness and integrity of life and concentrated on a kind of angelism in contemplation. . . . Now that I am a little less perfect I seem to have a saner perspective.[97]

This work underwent four revisions over the next decade. In the first he made reference to Eastern religions as contributing helpful insights for Christians into contemplative experience for the first time. Shortly after he began this work Merton took up the reading of Chuang Tzu's poems on the Tao, so that as this work progressed he was in a better position to evaluate the ways in which Eastern practice and thought might prove helpful to his own tradition.

One of the eight chapters of this series treats of specifically Christian Contemplation (Chapter III). It continues, from another perspective, his reflections on desert spirituality and the life of *quies*. Further, it complements his writings on Zen and Taoism, which were published during the ten years that this text was still under consideration, by presenting his views on the subject of contemplation from quite a different aspect than that taken in the Eastern books. Since he expressed his desire to see it published, any presentation of his teaching on this central theme of inner experience in order to do justice to his thought must make use of the whole of this important series and this chapter in particular.

The first assertion he makes is that in the biblical tradition what is at the base of all Christian mysticism is that man was created a contemplative. This is implied in the account of Paradise where Adam and Eve walked with God habitually and spoke with Him familiarly; they were at ease in their exchanges with him, simple and intimate. Merton follows St. Augustine's teaching that in the fall man was led astray and lost the simplicity of contemplation; he found himself in multiplicity and was troubled by the distractions attended upon existence in a complicated world. No longer was he at home in Paradise for which he was originally well suited. In God's presence he felt threat-

---

97. Shannon, op. cit., 113.

ened and so he found himself to be an exile, an alien in that world. He was even estranged from himself; he had to study himself, for now that he was no longer one with his Creator he was no longer at one with himself. To return to union with his Creator he must recover his own unity by rediscovering his true self. This recovery of the true self is possible only at God's initiative and historically that means in the person of Christ.

Merton develops at great length and in considerable detail the Patristic teaching on the Incarnation. It is only because Christ is truly God and truly man that we ourselves can return to the state for which we are made through the process of divinization. He points out that, if Athanasius gave so much stress to the true understanding of the Incarnation, it was not from some philosophical scruple; rather, he saw clearly that the whole work of salvation and sanctification depended on the fact that the Savior is divine as well as human. It is significant that this same Athanasius is the man who wrote the *Life of Antony* where the origins of the life of *quies*, the source of Hesychasm, is depicted in colorful detail. Merton here makes it abundantly clear that his own view of the contemplative life coincides in all essentials with the teaching of St. Paul and the Catholic fathers. He cites several texts of Maximus the Confessor, whom he had studied assiduously and whom he came to admire greatly.

> The superessential Word, clothing Himself at the time of His ineffable conception with all that is in our nature, possessed nothing human that was not at the same time divine. . . The knowledge of these things is indemonstrable, being beyond understanding and perceptible only to the faith of those who honor the mystery of Christ in the sincerity of their heart. (*Ambigua*, PG 91:1053)

> The mystery of the Incarnation of the Word contains in itself all the meaning of the enigmas and symbols of Scripture, all the significance of visible and intelligible creatures. He who knows the mystery of the Cross and the Sepulchre (sic) knows the reason (logos) of all things. He who is initiated into the hidden meaning of the resurrection, knows the end for which, from the beginning, God created all things. (*Centuriae Gnosticae*, PL 90:1108)

God desires at all times to make Himself man in those who are worthy. (*Quaestiones ad Thalassium* PG 90:321)

The larger part of this same essay is devoted to showing how this doctrine is rooted in the New Testament, in the theology of St. Paul and that of St. John's Gospel, each of whom he cites extensively. His reading of St. Paul's teaching on the Holy Spirit, for instance, manifests Merton's chief concerns about inner transformation and life in the Spirit. He points out that the Spirit is given to the Church to preserve her in truth and charity, and also to each member to draw him into awareness of God's action in his own life. The presence of the Spirit impels the believer to confront the void he finds within his own center when he is alone, to penetrate into it, and to discover there the loving mercy of God. Thus awareness of mystery comes to characterize the consciousness of the man of faith who meets God within. Living faithfully the implications of this discovery, the infinite depths of the self reveal themselves so that our nothingness paradoxically opens up the treasures of divine life from within.

Contemplation flows naturally from such a return to the hidden self. This is a central feature of Merton's insights into the contemplative experience. The contact with the sacred prepares the way for accepting one's true self, and experience of this inmost self is associated with a sense of a holy presence. This leads Merton to assert that

> The basic and fundamental problem of the spiritual life is the acceptance of our hidden and dark self, with which we tend to identify all the evil that is in us. We must learn by discernment to separate the evil growth of our actions from the good ground of our soul. And we must prepare that ground so that a new life can grow up from it within us beyond our knowledge and beyond our conscious control.[98]

Obviously, such a preparation of the heart represents an active disposition of the individual to respond receptively to any gift of contemplation that the Spirit may bestow. Thus Fr. Louis's doctrine on contemplation includes elements of psychology as

---

98. Shannon, op. cit., 42.

well as a spiritual anthropology that is at once profound and dynamic. He presents contemplation as the activity of a person who becomes whole in his humanity through seeking intimate union with God. Merton thus gave a fresh life to the word *contemplation* and to the ideal of a contemplative life that continues to speak to the minds and hearts of Cistercian monks today and which has a broad appeal to persons living in our own modern world.

VI. CONTEMPLATION AND RECOVERY OF LIKENESS

Father Louis Merton became increasingly aware of the need to treat the whole area of contemplative prayer in a fresh manner. His dissatisfaction with his approach to this topic in earlier writings, notably in the short work *What Is Contemplation?* and then in his widely read book *Seeds of Contemplation*, led him to return repeatedly to this subject and to revise his presentation in keeping with his more profound experiences of prayer and his broader knowledge of the spiritual life of other people, especially through teaching the young monks in his community. Thus he quite deliberately undertook to give renewed vigor to the term *contemplation*, and to make it more accessible to the people of his time. He speaks of this in 1962 in the Preface to *New Seeds of Contemplation*.

> As a result of this new perspective, many questions confronted the writer on taking up this old work again. Not least was the very use of the word *contemplation*. It is a misleading word in many respects. It raises great hopes that are all too likely to be illusory because misunderstood. It can become almost a magic word, or if not magic, then inspirational, which is almost as bad.[99]

Actually, Merton's earlier approach in this area of contemplative prayer had been more helpful to large numbers of people than his later criticism would suggest. It is useful to take note of some instances of people who profited from his writings on the

---
99. Thomas Merton, *New Seeds of Contemplation* (New York: New Directions Press, 1962) x.

topic to a point where it decisively changed their lives. One became an author himself who has written insightfully on the life of prayer. In the Introduction to his recently published book, *Thomas Merton's Paradise Journey,* (Cincinnati, Ohio 2000), Monsignor William Shannon tells the story of how reading Merton's writings on contemplation changed his life as a young priest. His account illustrates dramatically Merton's ability to give fresh content and new understanding to the word *contemplation.* Merton gave *contemplation* a place in the vocabulary and in the lives not only of monks but also of persons living in our modern world.

> I remember the year *The Seven Storey Mountain* was published. It was 1948. I was a young Catholic priest, ordained five years. Contemplation, I can assure you, was not a word in my working vocabulary. I certainly had read about it. I knew about Saint John of the Cross and his lofty climb up Mount Carmel. I had also read about Saint Teresa of Avila and her glorious interior castle; but it never really dawned on me that that castle was a place for me to enter or the climb up Mount Carmel a journey that I could make. It was *The Seven Storey Mountain* and other Merton works that would follow that convinced me that contemplation might just be a possibility for me and for the people I ministered to as a priest. For me this was a wonderful awakening to a new dimension of human existence. It brought me a totally new perspective on how I was to live my life.[100]

Merton addressed laymen as effectively as he addressed priests and religious. Paul Wilkes, a novelist, published an account of Merton's opening a window into the contemplative life style, ordered to deep prayer.

> I surely was not alone when as a high school student in the 1950's I found in Merton a rich, appealing, Catholic voice with an authenticity with which I could identify. I was handed *The Seven Storey Mountain* by a solicitous Marianist brother librarian . . . Merton took me beyond the limited horizons of a parochial-school education to another

---

100. William H. Shannon, *Thomas Merton's Paradise Journey* (Cincinnati: St. Anthony Messenger Press, 2000) 1–2.

world, one in which God was a living presence and not merely a distant deity. . . . I wanted to meet Thomas Merton; he was my Catholic hero far more significant in my young life than the ephemeral men who wore the [sports] uniforms. . . .[101]

Wilkes, a professional literary man, was taken with Merton's writing not only because of its high literary quality but also due to a style that was able to convey a sense of intimate sharing of personal experience that spoke to the heart.

Merton would find a place in my heart—and in millions of hearts in the United States and in the many foreign countries where his books were translated—surely because he was a gifted writer. But it was more than that. You could read Merton again and again; his was a voice that was human, accessible. There was no phony piety or false religiosity about him, no easy answers. You knew of your own struggles to be good and decent and to come closer to God, and Merton did not mask his own trials. For he was not a writer covered over who had become a monk in order to study analytically a soul's progress, but a man on fire with God.[102]

Wilkes concludes that Merton's message derived its great impact from his "traveling directly to the heart of God," rather than insisting on secondary matters. Steeped in tradition he boldly reinterpreted it rather than allowed it to serve as mere convention that limited personal initiative and creativity. This is a shrewd and sensitive assessment, I believe. "Going straight to the heart of God" is a good description of contemplation.

Monsignor Shannon, after half a century of studying Merton, remarks that the Trappist monk was extraordinarily broad in his interests and readings; he wrote about many areas of human interest, from politics, war and peace to Shaker theology, cargo cults of primitives and the Blessed Trinity.

Yet, if one takes a broad look at his writings, it can be said, I think, that contemplation was the explicit theme, or at

---

101. Paul Wilkes, *Boston College Magazine* (Winter 1999) 32.
102. Ibid., 33.

least the implied background, of most everything that Merton wrote. It was the cloud by day and the fire by night. . . . Contemplation was not one of many topics in Merton's field of vision, it was the focal point: the point he frequently and regularly "zoomed in" on. It was the *pointe vierge* he speaks of in *Conjectures of a Guilty Bystander*, the center from which his reflections on the human condition came forth and the goal to which they returned.[103]

"Contemplation," he goes on to add, "was at the center of his thinking about God and about prayer. It was also the starting point of his anthropology." An anthropology like Merton's that gives considerable scope to the unconscious goes far to account for the influence of his writing exerting interest on a wide variety of persons in our Western culture. Our society has integrated in a popular version many insights deriving from the personal unconscious as described by Freud, and to a lesser extent the concepts of the collective unconscious as Jung presented it.

Merton was sharply conscious of the central role of contemplation in his writings as well as in his life. He states as much in a letter written in 1959.

> I have just finished another book, *The Inner Experience*—a wider, deeper view of the same thing, contemplation, with more reference to Oriental ideas. There is to me nothing but this that counts, but everything can enter into it.[104]

Merton felt that the word *contemplation* needed a particularly nuanced treatment if it was not to cause misunderstandings. His early writing on contemplation in *Seeds of Contemplation* reflected the too narrow awareness of a young and enthusiastic convert who was still absorbed in the work of following up the grace of his own conversion and early formation as a Cistercian monk. He expressed his self-criticism and stated his new perspective in a Preface to the third edition. He modifies the title, calling it *New Seeds of Contemplation*, because of the extensive additions that display a much wider conception of the contem-

---

103. *Thomas Merton's Paradise Journey*, 7.
104. Thomas Merton, *The Courage for Truth*, edited by Christine M. Bochen (Farrar, Straus & Giroux, 1993) 63.

plative life and bear witness to a more personal and more profound experience of God and the mysteries of faith. His own words sum up his mind at the time of its publication.

He remarks first that this third revision of his work expanded it appreciably and was appearing some twelve years after the first and second redactions of this text, that is to say, from December 1949, the time of the second redaction, to 1962. This work had been a phenomenal success when it first appeared in 1949, selling 40,00 copies in four months and was reprinted ten times. Merton revised it the same year it appeared, by which time it had already had six printings. He was not satisfied with its too restricted views and relatively narrow horizons. He goes on to explain why he now produces a second, much more extensive revision.

> When the book was first written, the author had no experience in confronting the needs and problems of other men. The book was written in a kind of isolation, in which the author was alone with his own experience of the contemplative life. And such a book can be written best, perhaps only, in solitude. The second writing has been no less solitary than the first: but the author's solitude has been modified by contact with other solitudes; with the loneliness, the simplicity, the perplexity of novices and scholastics of his monastic community; with the loneliness of people outside any monastery; and with the loneliness of people outside the Church. . . . [105]

His earlier writing, while reflecting a depth of experience and conviction and proving very helpful to many, was too intellectual and too much conformed to accepted ways of conceiving and presenting the experience of God to satisfy Merton for long. Others too had criticized him for being too elitist, for example, as if only monks could actually be contemplatives. Merton came to agree with his critics; he could learn from capable people who honestly expressed their disagreements. And so we find that in this revision he gives greater importance to *experience*.

---

105. Thomas Merton, *New Seeds of Contemplation* (New York: New Directions Press, 1961) ix–x.

He also wrote for an enlarged audience, persons who were not in the Church, even non-Christians, who could be reached by a work on contemplation that gave much scope to the natural endowments of the person as well as to the supernatural.

As he developed his views of contemplation, he increasingly stressed the *apophatic* quality of mystical prayer. Already in his first work dealing formally with this topic *What Is Contemplation?* he had demonstrated his decided preference for the way of darkness over the way of light; his later works progressively explored the implications of the dark knowledge of God that leads ever deeper into the divine mystery of the uncircumscribed God. What this means is that the most important knowledge derived from contemplation is that God is essentially unknowable; the truer one's perception of Him, the more profound the darkness in which He dwells.

As a result of his apophatic convictions, Merton teaches that what remains dark, obscure, only vaguely known, and yet is powerfully influential on the acting and perceiving subject, is what is the most precious element in the gift of contemplation. Merton's ideas on contemplation are analogous to psychic reality as it has been observed and described in the clinic and in everyday life. He explores an unconscious ground that gives rise to all kinds of forms and actions as its energies are translated into human expression whether in prayer or in action.

Merton's anthropology and, more specifically, his teaching of the central role of the true self and his descriptions of its nature, grows out of his concept of the apophatic quality of contemplation and remains in dialectical relation to the experience of God as unknowable in His essence. As he came to experience the mystery of God's infinitude and the dazzling darkness of the mind that encounters the uncircumscribable God, he realized increasingly the role of the transcendent self.

In contrast with this true self, the empirical ego, operating within the sphere of the finite, and so necessary to functioning in the everyday world, is seriously limited in its capacity for perceiving spiritual realities. The empirical ego quickly becomes a barrier to the deep knowledge of the Divine Persons, who are unlimited in nature, and not confined by any form. The fact that

Merton gives such a decisive role to this component of the human person, accessible in principle to everyone, anchors his contemplative theology in the concrete. This feature of his thought has the effect of giving substance to the inner life and contributed to making it seem plausible to many contemporaries of a more sophisticated and reflective turn of spirit to pursue seriously a life style that includes contemplation as an important and regular practice.

Merton himself underwent a transformation as he lived in his monastery with his fellow monks. The graces he received at prayer made him aware of a more existential approach to God, less confined within the fixed limits of dogmatic formulations and scholastic definitions. As Karl Rahner was to point out, every dogmatic definition represents a limit in one context and in one dimension, but is, at the same time, the starting point for a new direction leading to fresh insights into the divine mystery. This principle of legitimate evolution in the Church's appropriation of the content of faith applies also to the individual believer's growth in the Spirit. It finds an exemplary instance in the person of Merton who came to the conviction that he was called by God to open up new ways and broader horizons for his Order and for the Church as a whole.

He understood well that his contribution was to be precisely in the area of spiritual and human experience, as a monk and a poet endowed with gifts of nature and of prayer in the Spirit. His evolution took on a new momentum when he was given the responsibility of *Magister Spiritus, (Spiritual Teacher),* for the junior professed at Gethsemani in 1952. Since this took place shortly before I made my simple vows and became a member of that group, I can bear witness to the dedication he brought to this charge. He himself became aware of the impact that his relation with these students had on his views concerning the monastic way, the need of reform, and even on the experience of God. He wrote the book *No Man Is an Island* in these years and dedicated it to the students whom he taught and from whom he learned to enter a land of new horizons. He describes his way of envisaging the spiritual life with reference to his concept of the essential nature of the human person.

> I consider that the spiritual life is the life of man's real self, the life of that interior self whose flame is so often allowed to be smothered under the ashes of anxiety and futile concern. . . . The life of the spirit, by integrating us in the real order established by God, puts us in the fullest possible contact with reality—not as we imagine it, but as it really is. It does so by putting us in contact with our own real selves and placing them in the presence of God.[106]

This characteristic of his spirituality also links Merton closely with St. Bernard of Clairvaux who, centuries before, based his spirituality on an anthropology that likewise included a hidden structure within a recognizable and knowable reality. In his essence, Bernard maintains, man is best understood as being incomplete at present due to an invisible, unconscious, lost likeness to the Person in whose likeness alone he finds completion and happiness. This likeness remains as an unknown potential, at present covered over by sin, waiting to be activated by grace and the choice of the subject. For even in his present state, in which this likeness remains hidden in obscurity, the structural image of God in which he is created remains essentially intact in the form of *liberum arbitrium,* free choice. In the measure that the person returns to his inner self and becomes acquainted by experience with God, so he grows in self-knowledge. He begins to recognize how unlike the Holy One he finds himself. This consciousness of his distance from his divine Prototype fills him with a sense of anguish. He becomes as well more sensitive to the various miseries that beset him in this mortal and finite existence, for he knows himself as made for the immortal and eternal One whose image he bears within, covered over by his passions and ignorance.

While Merton's doctrine of man is far from being a copy of Bernard's anthropology, it is animated by a similar dynamic insight into the unconscious depths of the human person. The prominence that the 20th-century monk gives to the real self represents a legitimate development of the image/likeness role in the spirituality of the 12th-century Cistercian abbot.

---

106. Thomas Merton, *No Man Is an Island* (New York: Harcourt, Brace and Company, 1955) ix.

Bernard drew attention to the dimension of the person that is always operative, although functioning at only a fraction of its potential, the *liberum arbitrium* he calls it. *Free choice*, a literal translation, can be misleading if we think of it only an operation of the will when, in fact, it includes the mind and implies knowledge and understanding. Bernard analyzes free choice in fastidious detail distinguishing carefully its function from other activities. It is not the same as free counsel, which advises what is more expedient and useful for him; nor does it coincide with the pleasurable; rather its province is to judge what is *licit* and what is not. Thus, he points out, while we do have free choice we do not possess *liberum consilium, free counsel* by which we follow what is fitting naturally, nor, do we possess *liberum complacitum*, for we do not find pleasant all that judgment tells us is good. He considers it imperative to have as full and concrete a grasp of this power as we can manage, for it is a faculty that constitutes us in the very image of God. It includes not only choice but also active reasoning in the service of discernment, as he implies when he associates it with the act of judgment.

> We believe that the free choice is to take its name only from this liberty by which it is free to the will to judge itself to be good if it consents to the good, or evil if it consents to evil. Only by willing in either case does it feel itself to consent. . . . For choice is a form of judgment.[107] (*De Gratia et Libero Arbitrio* IV.11 PL 182:1007)

St. Aelred of Rievaulx, who is known as the Bernard of the North, following in the wake of his mentor, states that he also envisages this faculty as fundamental for spirituality. He sees it as occupying the critical center of the soul, with the flesh and its appeal on one side and, on the other, the call of the spirit. Like his mentor, the Abbot of Clairvaux, he is explicit in including the act of judgment in its operation.

> Free choice is indeed the soul's force or nature, or whatever other term can be found for that power in man whereby, not without the judgment of reason, he consents

---

107. *De Gratia et Libero Arbitrio* IV.11 PL 182:1007.

to anything whatever. It is not the actual consent to this or that, to good or evil, but that power by which one consents. . . . Consent is indeed an action of the soul, but free choice is a natural power of the soul, by which it gives consent, possessing implanted within itself a judgement by which it chooses the object of consent.[108]

The early Cistercians pointed to the invisible depths of the inner man and gave large portions of their attention to describing the structure of the human person. They did so in order to lead their audience to and recognize with greater clarity the true nature of their being and to attend more earnestly to its cultivation. It seems to me that one purpose they had in mind was to encourage their readers to enter into their inner world and become aware of the operation of those inner faculties that in their operation decide their worth and the meaning of their life.

For someone to recognize that he is capable of acting freely and so to give the meaning he chooses to his life is to become conscious of possessing a transcendent dignity. Without this consciousness, his transcendent dignity lies dormant and he cannot have confidence that he can attain to God Himself. To experience our freedom of choice in its openness to the divine is to discover within oneself a concrete basis for hope and a center from which one can become an active agent in working out one's potential. The doctrine of the hidden image and the potential for the likeness, so much stressed in Cistercian tradition, is a strong incentive to devote one's time and energy to the search for the experience of God which alone can satisfy the human heart. To know God is to regain the likeness since like can be known only by like.

Merton employs a language that revitalizes the concept of a hidden center that is the spring from which a person's life ever flows forth and whose source is the very Spirit of God who abides within its recesses. He invites his readers to look into their own heart and discover for themselves the fountain of living water welling up to eternal life. His anthropology is then a modern version of the Cistercian view of man as the image of God whose

---

108. *The Mirror of Charity*, I.29, (Kalamazoo: Cistercian Publications, 1990) 103.

perfection results from recovering the likeness to his creator and redeemer.

I wish to further develop an understanding of Merton's use of the concept "the true self." Interestingly, at the end of his introduction to his translation of the *Sayings of the Fathers*, he draws a conclusion that certainly would not occur to most students of that literature. Though the texts themselves do not formulate their message in these terms, he finds in their recorded stories and saying indications of *the central role of the true self in the work of transformation*. He considers this as their chief message to us today. He urges his readers to make it our task to enter upon this work of the heart by making the discovery of our own true self. There is no better way to profit from the example and sayings of the Fathers of the Desert.

> We cannot do exactly what they did. But we must be as thorough and as ruthless in our determination to break all spiritual chains, and cast off the domination of alien compulsions, to find our true selves, to discover and develop our inalienable spiritual liberty and use it to build, on earth, the Kingdom of God.[109]

One of the effects of contemplation is the strengthening of the depths of the personality that can then reorganize the subject's consciousness under the dominance of the knowledge imprinted in the soul. This has the ultimate effect of decompartmentalizing the psychic contents. The result is an increased sense of unity and simplicity of the inner world. This unity and simplicity is the ultimate result because in certain instances the immediate result is paradoxical in that, as a result of such a profound inner impact, one may experience an emergence of hidden emotional conflicts and the anxiety they produce. The contemplative experience of discovering one's true self has a decided impact on the identity of the one practicing such prayer, and Merton gives considerable attention to this fact. In order fruitfully to receive the gift of contemplation, one must be prepared for it by having a healthy sense of identity in the first place.

109. *The Wisdom of the Desert*, 24.

A sense of identity in our society cannot be taken for granted. One of the most common defects observed in modern persons is that of being subject to various false selves. It is not too much to say that practically everyone labors under this distorted sense of self to some extent. Merton referred to this problem in *Seeds of Contemplation:* "Everyone of us is shadowed by an illusory person, this false self."[110] In the early stages of the ascetic life, various problems arise from unrealistic expectations and demands imposed by this false self. It becomes necessary to identify these distortions of the false self for what they are and then work to refashion one's expectations and demands in keeping with one's real capacities, interests, and values with the aid of a director and possibly a counselor. The false self causes one to act a role, conforming to self-imposed demands, often enough projected upon those whose approval is sought. The novice in such a state acts as he thinks a monk is supposed to act, but has no inner sense of his own center from which his personal way of living emanates. Obviously, there can be no contemplative prayer for such a one. One must have a personal center, enter the heart, and discover there who one truly is in the depths in order to respond to the presence of God within the soul.

Of its very nature the true self is incommunicable; it evades sharply outlined definition. It is not some portion of our being but, as Fr. Louis puts it,

> It is our entire substantial reality itself, on its highest and most personal and most existential level. It is like life and it is life; it is our spiritual life when it is most alive. It is the life by which everything else in us lives and moves. It is in and through and beyond everything that we are. If it is awakened, it communicates a new life to the intelligence in which it lives so that it becomes a living awareness of itself . . .[111]

One of the features of this self to which Merton repeatedly adverts in various of his works is that it is not an object we possess; rather it is pure subjectivity, the whole person alive, receptive,

---

110. *New Seeds of Contemplation,* 28.
111. Thomas Merton, "The Inner Experience," *Cistercian Studies* 18 (1983) 5, 6.

and responsive to God and to His communications. This central focus of our being flourishes best where there is simplicity, purity of heart, detachment, and humility. There are degrees of its manifestation, to be sure. Most of our spiritual experience takes place in the derivative self, that is to say at a level that reflects something of the true self but which is not fully pervious to it. We can enter the interior places of the heart once we have cultivated a certain discipline and awareness, but there is no faculty, no technique that exercises direct control over the all-encompassing dimension of our being. It is highly responsive to grace; it is the place where God abides within and from which he communicates Himself to us.

Merton does indicate inner and outer behaviors that favor access to this true self. As indicated above, detachment and humility of heart, purity of life favor its development. Cultural elements such as poetry, myths, liturgical rites, archetypes, and symbols that stimulate the inner life contribute to the vitality of this self. Living in an environment that favors silence, solitude, and inner attentiveness supports the manifestation of this secret center of life within.

Since this true self is given with nature, it is a dimension of every human person. Like any other gift of nature it can be enhanced by practices that lead to its purification and development. In "The Inner Experience" Merton points to the meditation and ascetic practices of Zen as an instance of such training leading to *satori*, as the Zen masters call enlightenment. This is all to the good, but the Christian seeks union with God and the experience of His presence. That calls for grace; it is not within the power of the individual to achieve. But it is God's intent and desire to communicate Himself and to those whom He chooses He freely bestows such grace. St. Augustine provides Merton with texts that movingly witness to the way that God gives Himself to the one who seeks Him in this inmost sanctuary.

> Admonished by them (Platonic writings) to return to myself, I entered to my most intimate self, with you as my guide. I was able to do that for you were my helper. I entered and saw with some sort of eye of my soul, above the

same eye of my soul, above my mind, the Light unchangeable. . . And you beat back the weakness of my sight, radiating with great force, and I trembled with love and dread. And I found myself far from you in the region of unlikeness as I should hear your voice from on high: "I am the food of adults; grow and eat me. You will not change me into you, but you will be changed into me."[112]

Merton did not include these last two sentences when he cited this passage, but both are particularly significant here. First, one of the effects of entering into the realm of the true self is to become keenly aware of the great distance between God and the self, and to know oneself with a new kind of insight so as to recognize how unlike God one is. Only God's initiative can bridge this vast distance. The other point brought out here is that it is by the activation of the true self, the most intimate self as Augustine phrases it here, that the process of inner transformation is most effectively carried through. *"You will be changed into me,"* God says.

In pursuing his attempts to delineate the features of the true self and its relation to the Christian God, Merton approvingly discusses Tauler's teaching on this subject. Often in other writings Merton will make use of the Rhenish Dominican's vocabulary in referring to this transcendent self: The inmost "I" is the *ground* or *center* or *apex* of the soul. When he enters into this inmost temple, Tauler states, the subject

> finds God dwelling and at work. Man then comes to experience God not after the fashion of the senses and of reason, or like something that one understands or reads. . . but he tastes Him, and enjoys Him like something that springs up from the "ground" of the soul as from its own source.[113]

Elsewhere Tauler describes how God can suddenly act upon this "ground" with His special graces and transmute it wholly. He indicates how, by causing a profound turmoil in this deep-

---

112. *Confessions* VII.X.16 PL 32, 742
113. Sermon on Thursday before Palm Sunday cited by Merton in "The Inner Experience," 9.

est level of the self, this immediate contact with God prepares the ground for a real transformation. He describes the result from the spiritual, rather than the psychological, perspective.

> From this passage of the Spirit is born a great tumult in the soul. And the more this passage has been clear, true, unmixed with natural impression, all the more rapid, strong, prompt, true, and pure will be the work which takes place in the soul, the thrust which overturns it; clearer also will be the knowledge that the man has stopped on the path to perfection. The Lord then comes like a flash of lightning; he fills the ground of the soul with light and will to establish himself there as a Master Workman. As soon as one is conscious of the presence of the Master, one must in all passivity abandon the work to Him.[114]

Tauler stresses that this inmost place becomes wholly receptive when God takes such initiatives. Such encounters with God are healing. It is easier for us today than it was in Tauler's age to see in greater detail just how this healing affects the various psychological levels of the soul and the character of one who experiences such a grace. Such an experience confronts the individual with those hidden character defects that had earlier escaped his notice. In this way it places him in a position where he can more effectively modify them for the better. This represents a specific instance of how the experience of God can put us in a position to make more effective use of modern depth psychology to profit more fully from spiritual graces. Such clearer insight allows for a more efficacious participation in the process of transformation in all its aspects, as it effects the alteration of the habits of the psyche, the gradual liberation from evil habits, growth in virtue, and, finally, culminating ideally in the integration of the whole person in the service of union with God.

Merton was marked by his contact with Tauler who contributed to his insights regarding the process of transformation, the role of the true self, and the dark knowledge of God given when a man discovers God acting in this dark center of his being. As he gained more experience of prayer, as he studied and

---

114. *II Sermon for the Holy Cross* cited in ibid., 9–10.

observed more widely the psychological and spiritual make up of people, both Eastern and Western, Merton would periodically return to these themes of the nature of contemplation, the true self, the false self, and the ways to attain to a purer, truer knowledge of God in view of a more perfect union with Him. In addition to pursuing these insights further in various works written in the last years of his life, he incorporated these insights into what is probably his most influential book on the spiritual life, *New Seeds of Contemplation*. As a result, this work, published 38 years ago, is still in print and being read by men and women, monks and nuns of our Order among them, striving to deepen their spiritual lives and to cultivate their capacity for contemplation. The teaching that this spiritual classic embodies, by building upon the solid foundation of a transcendent anthropology, represents an adaptation of our Cistercian heritage to the needs and aspirations of many persons in our times.

VII. LOVE, TRANSFORMATION, AND THE NEW MAN

"We must now speak about where our love begins, for we have already said where it is consummated."[115] Thus does St. Bernard introduce his analysis of love and the various stages of development through which the lover must pass if he is to achieve the purpose for which he is created. Thomas Merton, time and again in his writings and teaching on spirituality, took up this same theme of love. He analyzed and described it in its beginnings, its transformations, and its full expansion until it is consummated in that complete union with God that alone satisfies the human person. In this vast area of the nature and forms and functions of love he proved to be a worthy modern follower of the early Cistercians. It was not only Bernard of Clairvaux who wrote extensively on this topic of love but William of St. Thierry and St. Aelred of Rievaulx also wrote at length and repeatedly on the subject. If we would understand Merton's contribution to presenting the place of love in Cistercian spirituality in a fresh, updated form that is adapted to the consciousness and sensibility of persons living in our times, we must first have a fairly definite concept of what our Fathers had to say on the subject and, no less importantly, why they wrote about it in such detail.

What purpose, then, does Bernard and the other two Cistercian authors have in identifying and describing in detail the kinds and degrees of love? They do not tell us explicitly, but it would seem that they are convinced that to know that there are higher degrees of love is itself a stimulus to seek to realize in one's own life the more perfect kind. If they give a rather

---

115. *De Diligendo Deo*, VI. 22 PL 182:987.

extended description of each stage, it is because the more clearly a person envisages his goal, the more effectively he can take the measures necessary to attain it and the more he will be encouraged to undertake the arduous task of attaining to the purity of love. Certainly, this was Merton's purpose in writing at such length and with such specific detail on this same theme in any number of his writings.

The knowledge of the various kinds and stages of love, to be sure, does not suffice of itself. One can understand a great deal about its nature, its demands, and its benefits and yet not advance interiorly in its ways. In order to profit from such knowledge a person must put into practice the specific kind of action that is characteristic of that degree of love which one already possesses.

Following the classic teaching of the Ancients, Bernard points out that love is but one of four natural affections, the other three being fear, joy, and sadness.[116] The fact that the Abbot of Clairvaux chooses to describe human progress and fulfillment precisely in terms of the quality of love is itself a strong statement concerning the primacy of this affection and an indication of the radical importance he assigns to it. In his opinion, the purer, the nobler, the more ardent the love that motivates and characterizes the individual the more successful is that person's life.

That he describes the purpose of monastic life, indeed of all human living, as being essentially a process of profound change in the quality of one's love until it attains to its perfection means that Bernard views our human condition as engaged in a dynamic transformation of what is deepest in the person. The driving force of this process is love in movement, a desire for that state of being which unites one with God.

The work of the spiritual life is the radical remaking of the whole person. Spiritual progress is not simply a question of learning new habits, of adapting to a different life-style, of developing new skills. It is a matter of a new creation, one that affects the self at its highest point, of refashioning its deepest being and of redirecting its energies as they arise from its most hidden center. These are all precisely points that Merton makes in the course of his efforts to provide for renewal of formation and of life style in our Order.

---

116. *De Deligendo Dei*, VIII. 23; cf. also *Sermo II.3 in Capite jejunii*.

Such a view of the human person is derived from the New Testament. Jesus had taught Nicodemus the necessity of being born anew, from above, by the action of the Spirit of God upon the individual. He spoke of becoming perfect as the heavenly Father is perfect. St. Paul developed a theology based on this dynamic vision of human rebirth into a new sphere where God is at the center, permeating all. He realizes that such a process amounts to a whole new creation and so he speaks of it as a transformation (μεταμορφόομαι in the original). Although he uses this word but twice, it is decidedly one of the most momentous terms in his spiritual vocabulary, as appears from this passage and the other instance where he employs it. The transformation he has in mind is a life long process that culminates in the formation of a person so constituted that he is capable of participating happily in the very life of God himself.

> I exhort you, therefore, brothers, through the mercy of God, to present your bodies as a living sacrifice, holy, pleasing to God, your rational service. And *do not be conformed to this world; rather be transformed in the newness of your mind,* so as to determine for yourselves what is the good and pleasing and perfect will of God. (Rom 12:1-2)

The second text introduces further the role of the Spirit and the contemplation of the glory of God revealed in Christ in this transformation process.

> The Lord is the Spirit. Where the spirit of the Lord is, there is freedom. For our part, let us all, beholding as in a mirror with unveiled faces the glory of the Lord, be transformed from glory to glory as by the Spirit of the Lord. (2 Cor 3:8)

The only other times this verb is used in the New Testament are in regard to the Transfiguration of Jesus as recounted by Saints Mark and Matthew. In both instances the text reads: "And he was transfigured before them" (Matthew 17:2; Mark 9:2).

In another passage St. Paul uses another term to express the same concept of a radical restructuring of the individual in such a way as to result in a conformity to the archetype, the glorified Christ.

> For our citizenship is in heaven from where we shall also receive the Lord Jesus Christ who will transform

(μετασχηματίσει) the body of our lowliness so that it is fashioned like the body of his glory, according to the energy of the one who is able to subject all things to himself. (Phil 3:18)

In each of these five passages held up to our faith is the final form of the whole person at the end-time, when the Lord introduces those who have been modeled upon him into the presence of the glory of his Father. Jesus' transfiguration is a foreshadowing of his post-resurrection glorification; it also is a promise of our own, in so far as we participate by our lives in his passion and death.

The proper task of the monk is "the work of the heart," that "place" at the center of his being where he encounters the living God and receives the graces needed day by day for the great work of deification. Fervor and dedication are prominent features of St. Bernard's spirituality; so is the desire for an elevated life of pure prayer which is sustained by the ascetic practices that have always been integral with the more contemplative forms of prayer. He too had been taught by the Gospels and St. Paul that to attain to our full promise and arrive at the fulfillment of our aspiration for the truly happy life we must undergo a profound restructuring, a transformation of our whole self. He gives expression to this realization in his Sermons on the Canticle.

> *We have seen his glory, glory as of the only begotten of the Father* (John 1:14). For totally benign and truly paternal is the glory that appears in this way. This glory does not oppress me although I look upon it with all my powers; rather I am imprinted by it. For contemplating it with unveiled face we are transformed into the same image from glory to glory as by the Spirit of the Lord (2 Cor.3:18). We are transformed when we are conformed. May it not happen that conformity to God be presumed by man in the glory of majesty and not rather in the modest subjection of his will.[117]

In a later Sermon Bernard returns to this same theme of transformation and develops it in the context of other images.

---

117. *Sermones in Cantica* 62.5 PL 183: 1078B, C.
117. *Sermones in Cantica* 71.4, 5 PL 183: 1123A, B.

Love, Transformation, and the New Man

When he (the good Father of the family) feeds us he is fed himself, I believe, and the food by which he is willingly nourished is our progress . . . . His food is my penance, his food is my salvation, his food is my very self. Does he not eat ashes as his bread? I, because I am a sinner, am ashes and so am eaten by him. I am eaten when I am rebuked, I am swallowed when I am instructed, I am boiled when I am changed, I am digested when I am transformed, I am united when I am conformed. Do not marvel at this. He eats us and he is eaten by us the more closely we are bound to him.[118]

Bernard's good friend William of St. Thierry too developed a strongly dynamic spirituality that saw the goal of the ascetic and contemplative life as a veritable reforming of the person. He uses a somewhat different vocabulary, but conveys essentially the same truth.

And so it happens that when we flee to him (God) there is no change in him, that is, in his nature, but we do change when we are made better from worse. Likewise when he begins to be our Father he does not change, but we are regenerated and become sons of God by the grace of him who gives us power to become sons of God. And when we are made sons of God our substance is transformed *(transmutetur)* for the better.[119]

Any number of other passages could be adduced from our Cistercian Fathers that bear witness to their dynamic understanding of the tradition that affirms the purpose of our way of life to be a radical transformation of our very being and not merely the adaptation to the subculture of the cloister. There are further texts treating of this subject under other aspects, such as divinization, that is, the highest expression of transformation, as in the well-known saying of St. Bernard: "Thus to be affected is to be divinized *(Sic affici deificari est)*" in *De diligendo Deo 10*. St. Aelred, Isaac of Stella, and other Cistercian writers have left us texts that reveal the same conviction that the purpose of our

---

118. *Sermones in Cantica* 71.4, 5 PL 183:1123A, B.
119. *Aenigma Fidei* PL 180:424B.

life is the radical engagement of our whole being in the work of the inner man, under the influence of the Spirit, until we are refashioned in the likeness of Christ Jesus, our Lord and Savior.[120]

As he read the Cistercian Fathers, Merton quickly came to see the dynamic center of their concept of monastic life was this process of radical restoration of the primitive likeness to God. Man is created in the pattern fashioned after the hidden, mysterious nature of God Himself. Merton came to understand that, having rediscovered the fundamental role of this dynamic concept of monastic life and entering into its spirit, he needed to live according to its severe ascetic demands. Before long he became convinced he was called upon to reformulate it by describing the process as he had experienced it in his own monastic life, so as to communicate it to other monks and persons of all ways of life in the living language of our own times.

Merton repeatedly emphasized the need to preserve and emphasize those practices that the tradition has always considered essential for the attainment of this goal of recovering the likeness to Christ through transformation. To cite one instance of many, in his diary entry for September 6, 1948, he describes his sense of restlessness and inner conflict arising largely from the consequences of the prominence that his recently published autobiography had brought him. His reflections on this situation are an attempt to clarify his interior vision of his vocation as a monk.

> To make a Rule the whole meaning of my existence is not enough. To make an Order, a spiritual tradition, the center of my life is not enough. Contemplation is not enough: by itself it is not enough of an ideal. The complete gift of myself to Christ—transformation—total simplicity and poverty—these are some of the things I need.[121]

In the subsequent years of his early priestly activity as a teacher and spiritual guide of the scholastics he continued to expand and deepen his grasp of this process. His further insights led to the revision of his earlier work, serving to complete rather

120. Cf. *Dictionaire de Spiritualité* III.1405 ff s.v. *Divinisation*.
121. *Entering the Silence*, 229.

than to correct the earlier concept he had formed of this work of transformation. He gave to this new, expanded edition a fresh name, *New Seeds of Contemplation,* for the additions had considerably altered its general tone in the direction of showing that contemplation and the process of transformation is more accessible to all persons of good will than the earlier editions had conveyed.

Although he continued throughout his life to enlarge upon this theme of contemplative prayer and the process of transformation that the Greek Fathers especially called *deification,* the presentation of these matters as set out in *New Seeds of Contemplation* expressed views that remained essentially conformed to his experience and opinions down to the end of his life. *New Seeds* contains the essence of his contribution to the renewal of our Cistercian heritage in light of the signs of our modern times.

By stressing the role of love in contemplation, and by showing the necessity of arriving at pure love, Merton demonstrates that contemplation is not only for the more highly intelligent and cultivated. Love is more democratic than intelligence:

> The only true joy on earth is to escape from the prison of our own false self, and enter by love into union with the Life Who dwells and sings within the essence of every creature and in the core of our own souls. In His love we possess all things and enjoy fruition of them, find Him in them all.[122]

He examines the chief obstacle to this work of love, namely, the false self and identifies it by describing its nature and the characteristics of its operations.

> An illusory person shadows every one of us: "a false self."
> This is the man that I want myself to be but who cannot exist, because God does not know anything about him. And to be unknown of God is altogether too much privacy.
> My false and private self wants to move outside the reach of God's will and God's love—outside of reality and outside of life. And such a self cannot help but be an illusion.[123]

---

122. *New Seeds of Contemplation,* 25.
123. Ibid., 34.

This is one of a number of passages where he describes this problematical agent that repeatedly gets in the way of anyone seeking spiritual advancement. Elsewhere he writes of the state of unlikeness that results from the influence of this intrusive self that keeps us from entering our own center and so into the place where God communicates most freely with us. He does not use the term "false self " but its active role is implied in the effects it produces.

> [W]hen that inmost "I" awakens he finds within himself the Presence of Him Whose image he is. . . . To anyone who has full awareness of our "exile" from God, our alienation from this inmost self, and our blind wandering in the "region of unlikeness," this claim can hardly seem believable.[124]

Later he describes the "false self" so that we can recognize its evil fruits when they appear and discern their cause.

> People who know nothing of God and whose lives are centered on themselves, imagine that they can only find themselves by asserting their own desires and ambitions and appetites in a struggle with the rest of the world. They try to become real by imposing themselves on other people, by appropriating for themselves some share of the limited supply of created good and thus emphasizing the difference between themselves and the other men who have less than they, or nothing at all.
> They can only conceive one way of becoming real: cutting themselves off from other people and building a barrier of contrast and distinction between themselves and other men.[125]

Mistaken identification with this false self, while causing a barrier between our real person and God, also results in our alienation from others and our inability to experience the goodness of creatures. Merton accordingly devotes a chapter of *New Seeds* to the question of identity in which he discusses at length the issue of becoming what God intended us to be in giving us our freedom. Our task is to employ this gift in such a way as to realize in

124. *The Inner Experience* I, 13.
125. Ibid., 47.

practice, day by day, that which accords with the deepest truth of our being.

> Our vocation is not simply to *be,* but to work together with God in the creation of our own life, our own identity, our own destiny. We are free beings and sons of God. . . . The seeds that are planted in my liberty at every moment, by God's will, are the seeds of my own identity, my own reality, my own happiness, my own sanctity.
> To refuse them is to refuse everything; it is the refusal of my own existence and being: of my identity, my very self.[126]

Subjection to the false self, living from a false identity without realizing most of the time that one's life is hollow at the core, is the fruit of sin. In the first instance it is the result of original sin, and like some other consequences of that fall, it is not removed by baptism, though the means of overcoming it are given by that sacrament. We must actively create the true self by a collaboration with God and thus gradually eliminate the scope of the falsity that we are born into and so readily accept without the help of grace. In this perspective the contemplative life is not only a search for union with God but, at the same time, the creation of the self I am to be for all eternity.

> Therefore there is only one problem on which all my existence, my peace and my happiness depend: to discover myself in discovering God. If I find Him I will find myself and if I find my true self I will find Him.[127]

This self, then, is not the product merely of nature, but of grace. "The only one who can teach me to find God is God, Himself alone." In these pages, then, Merton indicates how contemplation is a crucial element in the process of transformation that has a weighty significance for everyone. The fact that the experience of finding God in prayer has very specific effects on our sense of identity and so affects all our relations with the world, as well as with our Creator, tends to bring it into the sphere of the practical and so make it appear more accessible to people.

126. Ibid., 32–33.
127. Ibid., 36.

This feature of Merton's book accounts, in good part, I believe, for its continuing popularity. Contemplation somehow appears less esoteric when placed in such a context of the everyday changes that are determining the person we are and are becoming. The place of contemplation is found at the center of our own being.

> There exists some point at which I can meet God in a real and experimental contact with His infinite actuality. This is the "place" of God, His sanctuary—it is the point where my contingent being depends upon His love. Within myself is a metaphorical apex of existence at which I am held in being by my Creator.
>
> God utters me like a word containing a partial thought of Himself . . . if I am true to the thought of Him I was meant to embody, I shall be full of his actuality and find Him everywhere in myself, and find myself nowhere. I shall be lost in Him: that is, I shall find myself.[128]

Merton displays how contemplation makes crucial contributions to growth in self-knowledge, especially a heightened consciousness of the transcendent dimension of the person. He situates contemplative prayer more tellingly because more concretely, in the process of transformation. That this was his intention is clear from the following passages:

> To say that I am made in the image of God is to say that love is the reason for my existence, for God is love.
> Love is my true identity. Selflessness is my true self. Love is my true character. Love is my name. . . .
> To find love I must enter into the sanctuary where it is hidden, which is the mystery of God. And to enter into His sanctity I must become holy as He is holy, perfect as He is perfect. . . .
> If I am to be "holy" I must therefore be something that I do not understand, something mysterious and hidden, something apparently self-contradictory.[129]

Thus Merton leads up to what became increasingly a major aspect of his conception of contemplation: the hidden, mysteri

128. Ibid., 37.
129. Ibid., 60.

ous self which is discovered only in emptiness. This emptying out of what had previously supported us is a condition for possessing a strength that is rooted in the divine. It is a share in the emptying out that Christ embraced in his passion and death on the cross. This abasement is a response to God's love bestowed on us in Christ; it is itself a form of loving, terrible to nature but elevating and purifying. It is the path that Merton felt called upon to follow, however often he strayed from it, as his private journals and later writings attest.

He knew that he appeared to be a man of outstanding gifts, highly successful, influential with a life full of stimuli and friendships. Interiorly, however, his experience was, a large part of the time, that of inner desolation and solitude. His failings and faults, which he wrote about so frankly and at length, only intensified his sense of inner darkness. At times, as we shall see later, the sense of lostness was so strong it drove him to temporary infidelities to his vocation to solitude. He sought distraction and even love in ways that compromised his deepest convictions. But he returned repeatedly and, on the whole, with greater courage and conviction to this personal vision of his vocation as a search for holiness through a love that emptied him of all that is less than the absolute Love of God. He understood that engagement in this process of self-emptying was nothing less than a radical restructuring of his deepest self, a transformation of his whole being, from its very core.

> I who am without love cannot become love unless Love identifies me with Himself. But if He sends His own love, Himself, to act and love in me and in all that I do, then I shall be transformed, I shall discover who I am and shall possess my true identity by losing myself in Him.[130]

That this theme continued to hold a fascination for him is evident from many texts. In a poem Fr. Louis takes it up, varying the images and conceits with which he seeks to communicate this elusive and paradoxical mystical way, as he circles around the incommunicable experience of disconcerting emptiness.

130. Ibid., 63.

> When in the soul of the serene disciple / with no more Fathers to imitate Poverty is a success, It is a small thing to say the roof is gone: / He has not even a house . . . / What choice remains? / Well, to be ordinary is not a choice: / It is the usual freedom / Of men without visions.[131]

Transformation through growth in love is a prominent theme in Merton's highly praised poem, *Elegy for the Monastery Barn*, written in 1957. The occasion of this poem was the large conflagration at Gethsemani when the big barn, full of hay, burned down one evening after Vespers. [I might note here that I was present at the fire and afterwards, being the infirmarian, I treated Merton, who had entered the burning building, for a burned hand.] The real theme, however, is that of mystical transformation, as Michael Higgins points out.[132] The whole poem is one of singular charm and wit. I cite only the lines pertinent to our theme:

> Who knew her solitude? . . . / Who felt the silence, there, / The long hushed gallery / Clean and resigned and waiting for the fire? / Look! They have all come back to speak their summary: / Fifty invisible cattle, the past year / Assume their solemn places one by one. This is the little minute of their destiny. / Here is their meaning found. Here is their end . . . / Fly from the silence / of this creature sanctified by fire / Let no man stay inside to look upon the Lord! / Let no man wait within and see the Holy / One sitting in the presence of disaster / Thinking upon this barn His gentle doom![133]

Michael Higgins comments that

> The fire represents the "first–last hour of joy"' the culmination of the mystic's yearning for transcendence; the perfect image of the unified state. . . But this death by fire, this beatific transformation, is not gratuitous. Years of silence and solitude, of spiritual perseverance and monastic obedience preceded it.[134]

---

131. Thomas Merton, *The Collected Poems of Thomas Merton* (New York: A New Directions Book, 1977) 279.
132. *Heretic Blood*, 138–142.
133. *The Collected Poems*, 288–289.
134. *Heretic Blood*, 139–140.

Merton used this same image of fire as a symbol of transformation in other poems in which he attempted to communicate by images what he knew words could only point to, not adequately express. I cite two instances among his poems, which capture something of the spirit of what the Greek Fathers called *Theoria Physike*, that is, *the contemplation of God in nature*, that display Merton's exuberant response to the insights he received into this ongoing transformative process. The first, which is entitled *Freedom as Experience*, contains a particularly powerful image of love transformed in contemplation by flashes of light revealing something of the love of the Blessed Trinity.

> And then, as fires like jewels germinate / Deep in the stone heart of a Kaffir mountain, / So now our gravity, our new-created deep desire / Burns in our life's mine like an undiscovered diamond.[135]

The second bears the title *The Sowing of Meanings*. It is replete with images from nature that reveal the mystery of divine love hidden in the depths of created realities. Fire here is again the symbol of this recreation of the essence of the human person:

> For, like a grain of fire / Smoldering in the heart of every living essence / God plants His undivided power—/ Buries His thought too vast for worlds / In seed and root and blade and flower / . . . And our own souls within us flash, and shower us with light, / While the wild countryside, unknown, unvisited of men, / Bears sheaves of clean, transforming fire. / . . . And plants that light far down into the heart of darkness and oblivion, / Dives after, and discovers flame.[136]

At the end of his autobiography Fr. Louis had already spoken of the transformation he looked forward to completing as a trial by fire, as it were. Since he suffered severe burns on his body at the time of his death from electrical shock, it may not be too far-fetched to see in these final pages of his life's story an intimation of his prophetic insight into the meaning of his life's course and its end.

135. *Collected Poems*, 187.
136. Ibid., 188.

I hear you saying to me:

"I will give you what you desire. I will lead you into solitude. I will lead you by the way that you cannot possibly understand, because I want it to be the quickest way. . . .

"Everything that touches you shall burn you, and you will draw your hand away in pain, until you have withdrawn yourself from all things. Then you will be all alone.

"Everything that can be desired will sear you, and brand you with a cautery, and you will fly from it in pain, to be alone. . .

"You will be praised and it will be like burning at the stake. . . .

"And your solitude will bear immense fruit in the souls of men you will never see on earth. . . .

"That you may become the brother of God and learn to know the Christ of the burnt men."[137]

All of Merton's poetry could be analyzed for images that signify active participation in the work of discovering the true self. We are called to collaborate in our own transformation until we are truly formed in the image of the Son of God. Fire, light, and flowering are but a sampling of the rich imagery Merton calls upon to entice us to turn our attention and our energy to this most creative of all human endeavors, the process of transformation by which we are divinized and become children of God. But above all, it is love that supplies the energy requisite for this new creation and it is to a more thorough examination of this theme that I devote my final chapter.

---

137. *The Seven Storey Mountain*, 422–423.

VIII. THE NATURE AND MEANING OF LOVE

"Contemplation is the highest expression of man's intellectual and spiritual life. It is that life itself, fully awake, fully active, fully aware that it is alive." These opening words of Merton's classic on the contemplative life allow us to recognize immediately why he was so widely appreciated for his way of communicating the excitement he felt for the life of prayer. His words wake us up. They come as a call to live more fully. Such a manner of conceiving contemplation speaks to the heart of everyone with any love of life, with any youthfulness of spirit still throbbing within their breast. Not to make contemplation an important element in your life, he implies, is to miss out on what is best in your self. Do you want to live fully, to be wholly awake, energetic in your dealings? Then practice contemplation and you will makes discoveries for yourself what life can mean for you. With this first thought he tosses out, the author can hardly fail to get an attentive hearing for the rest of his message. He convinces us with these words because obviously he writes here with deep feeling, pouring out his whole self, his whole life into these lines.

How significant it is then to note that later on in his life, when he wrote on the great theme of love, Merton echoes these words concerning contemplation, elaborates them further, and gives added intensity to his expression, as if he were to say, "Here is a matter even more significant, more life-enhancing than contemplation, for it is the force that gives life to contemplation itself."

Life as love, contemplation, transformation of the inner self are three concepts pointing to realities that are increasingly interactive in Merton's writings. As his own development proceeded these realities took on ever more personal significance for him, that is to say, the meaning they came to contain was progressively filled out by his inner experience. As this revision of the concepts he had formed of love, contemplation and the process of transformation went ahead, the new content he gave to these terms represents, as I see it, his most fruitful contribution to the renewal of Cistercian spirituality in the post-Conciliar period down to our own times.

I have been considering the meaning he assigned to contemplation and his manner of conceiving of transformation. I would like to close this book by showing how his continuing interest in contemplation led him to a more elevated understanding of the concept of love, and a keener feeling for the process of transformation that effected the change from a more carnal to a more noble and purer love that is coextensive with a person's being and is identified with life itself in its fullest form.

The soul is so structured that there is an interface between contemplation, the true self and the way one loves. These three interact in a complex manner, at various levels of the inner life. There is a reciprocal dynamism in which energies are mutually and freely exchanged. The deeper self is affected by what takes place in contemplation and by the choices of love, and it in turn alters the way one experiences God and the manner one loves. Love itself provides the chief motive force in the demanding work of contemplation as in the arduous search for the discovery and development of the true self. This mutual influence is essentially what constitutes the process of transformation of the deepest self. This dynamic and spiritual view of human life as an active process of change at the core of the personality in the direction of greater purity of love and depth of insight is at the heart of Merton's teaching and, in very large part, accounts for his appeal to contemporaries.

If Merton defines contemplation in terms of life that is enhanced and elevated, he has his own opinion as to what authentic human life itself is. How he conceives of it, then, determines what he has in mind when he speaks of contemplation quite simply as life at its best. He wrote of this matter often, under a variety of aspects. Much depends in his spirituality and in his view of humanism upon his conviction that contemplation is not some esoteric method reserved for the few gifted and intelligent; rather, every human person is made to be a contemplative. The very structure of our being indicates this truth. We cannot become fully ourselves unless we pursue a contemplative life in one or other of its countless varieties.

Merton realized that this conviction concerning the normal development of a contemplative life for everyone holds vast implications for monastic formation. One of the most elaborately worked out statements on the nature of authentic human life made by Merton, in fact, occurs in the context of a consideration of the appropriate program and climate for the training of modern American youth to the monastic life. He was still treating of this issue even after he had resigned as novice master and took up the hermit life. He left this text in manuscript form, intending to complete it eventually after returning from his trip to Bangkok, a fact that suggests how much importance he continued to assign to this basic issue.

Merton was convinced at the time of this writing that the presuppositions for an adequate training and formation of mature monks accepted by the majority of those concerned with this first period of monastic life were out of touch with reality. Unless this could be recognized and fitting measures adopted in response to the situation as it has come to exist, frustration and even disaster would result for both the subjects and those charged with formation. In the course of dealing with many such postulants, novices, juniors, and even young solemn professed, and after analyzing their way of reacting to monastic initiation and training, his understanding of maturity and of the nature of genuine life itself fell into sharper focus. He states his views in the text that follows:

> The monastic life as it exists today often presupposes too much in the young postulant who seeks admission. It presupposes that he knows his own mind, and that he is capable of making a mature decision, that he has grown up, that he has received a liberal education. It is often discovered too late that such things cannot be taken for

> granted. Before the average youth of today is ready for monastic life, his senses, feeling and imagination need to be reformed and educated along normal natural lines. Americans under twenty-one who present themselves at the monastery gate are not usually full-blooded mature men with strong passions that need to be disciplined and mortified, but confused kids with a complex bundle of vague emotional fears and desires going in all directions at once. They are a pitiful mixture of pseudo-sophistication and utter vacuity. They are not only not ready for monastic life, they are not ready for any kind of life.[138]

Merton then essentially defines a mature human life as one capable of moral decision, firmly carried through and sustained because made by one whose sensibility, appetites, and values as he experiences them are clear to him. Life for the human person entails the development of appropriate feeling, imagination, and inner awareness of his values and state of soul. This implies a measure, however scanty, of self-knowledge of a concrete nature, including some accessibility to the true self. Merton continues his description of effects of technological society on youth, demonstrating especially how the resulting passivity and inertia are opposed to the requirements of the contemplative life. His final comments include a brief account of what he considers characteristic of life.

> Such a one (formed in passive, uncritical, inert attitudes) is not ready for the contemplative life because he is not ready for any kind of life. All life presupposes the ability to act, to work, to think for yourself, to break out of the cocoon, to get free of the womb. No life requires a more active or more intense formation, a more ruthless separation from dependence on exterior support, than the life of contemplation.[139]

Consequently, Fr. Louis saw that the challenge today is one of providing an adequate cultural formation, one that leads to the appropriate use of the senses, for those called to the Cistercian way of life. The education received by the average applicant today is, if anything, even less suited for the contemplative

---

138. *The Inner Experience*, VII, 32.
139. Ibid., 33.

The Nature and Meaning of Love 113

lifestyle. Knowledge is commonly factual and outer directed; it is not assimilated and possessed in a way that forms the person for the contemplative form of prayer and the style of life that supports it. Men are formed to be technicians and bureaucrats, Merton observes, and to prepare such persons for the monastic way monastic education must correct the defects arising by this distorted emphasis on functional formation. Such corrective efforts should include training to live in harmony with nature and a formation to literature and the arts. Those attitudes of mind and habits of acting they have learned are rather obstacles that first need to be cleared away and replaced by more properly mature and humane qualities

The monastic approach to this training is to enter into silence; to learn to deal with the manifold thoughts and temptations that assault the mind and imagination without having somebody else predigest them; to find one's own way in a situation of limited resources; to live in simplicity. No one can be expected to manage this without having inner resources already at hand.

> These things cannot be taken care of in a novitiate. There fasting, work, silence meditation, prayer, and liturgy, are all matters of rule and discipline. One practices them under relative tension, in an atmosphere of critical uncertainty. One is being "put to the test." But one is not ready for these projects under trying conditions unless he has first experienced them in a relaxed and precisely un-trying atmosphere. What is the use of "mortifying" your senses before you have had the pleasure of using them normally and innocently in the enjoyment of the good things of nature: before you have learned to *see* with your eyes, *taste* with your tongue, and *experience* reality with your whole being?[140]

Contemplation requires the training of the spiritual senses and this entails the gradual reformation and refinement of the five natural senses on which their operation is based. Merton here is in the tradition of Origen who had first developed a doctrine of the five spiritual senses.

140. Ibid., 38.

We can assert that that each member of the exterior man is found, under the same name, in the interior man. The exterior man has eyes, the interior man also is said to have eyes. . . in observing the divine precepts we acquire, in the order of the spirit, a more penetrating vision. The eyes of the interior man are more penetrating. . .[141]

The Alexandrian theologian reaffirms this view elsewhere. He bases himself on the Septuagint text of Proverbs 2:5, which differs from the Hebrew, in order to point out that this teaching is rooted in revelation.

"You discover the divine sense of perception." This sense, however, unfolds in various individual faculties: sight for the contemplation of immaterial forms. Hearing to hear sounds not occurring in the air. . . This sense for the divine was discovered by the prophets so that they saw, heard, tasted, and smelled in a divine manner. . .[142]

Origen's insights were prior in time and remained influential, but no less widely read and far more influential in the West was St. Augustine's more elevated literary presentation of the spiritual senses in their role of effecting the knowledge and love of God.

What is it that I love when I love you? Not the beauty of a body, not the harmony of time, nor the brightness of light- all of which are so agreeable to the eyes. Nor is it the sweet melodies of songs of all kinds, nor the fragrance of flowers and aromatic ointments, not sweet cakes and honey, nor arms inviting carnal embraces. These are not what I love when I love my God. And yet I do love a certain light, and a certain voice, a certain food and a kind of embrace when I love my God.[143]

William of St. Thierry took up this doctrine and elaborated further to form an important feature of the Cistercian tradition of contemplation.

141. *Entretien d'Origène avec Héraclide*, ed. Jean Scherer, Paris 1960, 88–90.
142. *Contra Celsum*, I. 48 S. Ch. 132 (1967) 205.
143. *Confessions* X. 6 PL 32: 782.

The Nature and Meaning of Love

For just as the body has five senses by which it is joined to the soul, with life mediating the union, so also the soul has five senses by which it is joined to God with charity mediating this union. So it is that the Apostle says: "Do not be conformed to this world, but be reformed in the newness of your sense, that you might know that the will of God is good, and pleasing and perfect" (Romans 12:2). Here he shows that through the bodily senses we grow old and are conformed to this world. But through the senses of the mind we are renewed in the knowledge of God, in newness of life, according to the will and good pleasure of God.[144]

William was not the only Cistercian to incorporate this doctrine of the spiritual senses into his spiritual teaching. In his *Sermones de Diversis*, X.2 St. Bernard of Clairvaux affirms his position on this question.

There is therefore life, truth, sense and charity of the soul. . . There is, if you observe carefully, to be found a variegated love, that is perhaps divided into five kinds corresponding to the five senses of the body.[145]

Abbot Baldwin of Ford developed in considerable detail a doctrine of all five spiritual senses. His elaboration of this topic is the most developed in the Cistercian repertory. He introduces this theme in the following lines:

When it is wonderfully united to God by the love of obedience, the soul lives and senses in him and by him, and it draws a sort of analogy with the things it knows through the bodily senses. Thus, by the grace of a most inward inspiration it senses God within itself and touches him spiritually by faith, smells him by hope, tastes him by charity, hears him by obedience, and sees him by contemplation.[146]

Hadewijch, the medieval Dutch poet and mystic, had read William of St. Thierry's treatment of the spiritual senses and followed his thought closely in her own spiritual teaching as she

144. "De natura et dignitate amoris," 22. Ed. M.-M. Davy. Paris, 1953, 95–96.
145. *PL* 18:568.
146. *Spiritual Tractates* I. IV (Kalamazoo: Cistercian Studies Publications, 1986) 118. Cf. PL 193:1192C for original Latin.

describes it in her Letter 80.[147] But it was St. Bonaventure who followed up with the most complete elaboration of this topic.

Thus, in insisting so heavily on the need for a soundly mature natural sensibility as a condition for a mature contemplative life, Merton is faithful to his program of restoring Cistercian life to its best spiritual traditions, and inserts himself in a venerable line of theologians and mystics. He recognized the importance of a sufficiently robust humanity to be able to fight against the manifold defenses of the false self so as to pursue the search for the true self where the monks can encounter God within. Dealing with this false self, then, was imperative, in his opinion, for the successful and proper training of men for the monastic way of life.

Perhaps the basis for maintaining this view of Merton's spirituality can be illustrated readily by examining his last book written on contemplation: *The Climate of Monastic Prayer*. He completed it shortly before his death so that it was published posthumously. He opens this work with a consideration of primitive monastic prayer and concludes that the early generation of monks prayed so very simply that one could ask what does such unimpressive prayer have to do with contemplation? His interpretation is a convincing one, based as it is on his appreciation of the fundamental role of the ordinary and of love in arriving at contemplation.

> They were careful not to go about looking for extraordinary experiences, and contented themselves with the struggle for "purity of heart" and for control of their thoughts to keep their minds and hearts empty of care and concern, so that they might altogether forget themselves and apply themselves entirely to the love and service of God.[148]

Their way of controlling thoughts was, he points out, by using the name of Jesus in prayer continuously until it was grounded in one's being. Meditating on the Passion was an extension of this same kind of prayer. Thus the ascetic struggle and the efforts to keep the Presence of God alive within blended

---

147. Cf. J. Van Mierloo Jr., sj, "Hadewijch en Wilhelm van St. Thierry," Ons Gestelijk Erf 3 (1929) 45–59.

The Nature and Meaning of Love

into the single, simple way of life that characterized the monks of Egypt and which has served as an ideal ever since for generations of men and women called to be their followers. But this way, while involving a separation from society, is not a flight from reality or from the people who live in the world. The contrary is the case: the monk's true vocation is to act as a leaven in the world by confronting its suffering and its difficulties head on, at the spiritual level which is where they take their origin.

> This is precisely the monk's chief service to the world: this silence, this listening, this questioning, this humble and courageous exposure to what the world ignores about itself—both good and evil. . . . The monk who is truly a man of prayer and who seriously faces the challenge of his vocation in all its depth is by that very fact exposed to existential dread.[149]

This concept of "existential dread" is central to various religious thinkers, Kierkegarrd and Heidegger among them. Merton appropriates this term dread to describe a crucial dimension of contemplation. As he develops his ideas in this context of dread and of contemplation and the monk's vocation in the modern world, Merton attains to a richness of expression that is at once lyrical and profound. If he speaks here in altogether convincing accents of the anguish and dread that arise from honestly facing the truth about oneself, it was because he had discovered the frightening force of these states of soul in his own heart. In words that I consider the most insightful and moving of the whole book, indeed, of his entire oeuvre, he describes the contemplative way as he came to understand it in his monastic setting.

> The monk who is truly a man of prayer. . . is by that very fact exposed to existential dread. He experiences in himself the emptiness, the lack of authenticity, the quest for fidelity, the "lostness" of modern man, but he experiences all this in an altogether different and deeper way than does man in the modern world, to whom this disconcerting awareness of himself comes rather as an experience of

---

148. Thomas Merton. *The Climate of Monastic Prayer*, Cistercian Publications (Washington, DC: Consortium Press, 1973) 21.

> boredom and of spiritual disorientation. The monk confronts his own humanity and that of his world at the deepest and most central point where the void seems to open out into black despair. . . .[150]

That Merton speaks here from experience is indicated in a letter where he wrote of what it would mean to follow his teaching on the spiritual life.

> If there is such a thing as "Mertonism," I suppose I am the one that ought to beware of it. The people who believe in this term evidently do not know how unwilling I would be to have anyone repeat in his own life the miseries of mine. That would be flatly a mortal sin against charity. I thought I had never done anything to obscure my lack of anything that a monk might conceive to be a desirable quality. Surely this lack is public knowledge, and anyone who imitates me does so at his own risk. I can promise him some fine moments of naked despair.[151]

We know from elsewhere in his Journals that he repeatedly had to struggle with the demands of his solitary path to contemplation, which, on occasion, were more than he could handle.

But if a monk's place in the modern world is to struggle with dread, a monk's life is also a testimony to hope as a gift of God's merciful grace. These words reflect a confidence and enthusiasm that express the newly acquired strength of one who, having descended to the depths of temptation, had experienced the mercy of God in a fresh and full commitment to his monastic vocation.

> The monk faces the worst, and discovers in it the hope of the best. From the darkness comes light. From death, life. From the abyss there comes, unaccountably, the mysterious gift of the Spirit sent by God to make all things new, to transform the created and redeemed world, and to reestablish all things in Christ.[152]

149. Ibid., 27.
150. Ibid., 37–38.
151. *The School of Charity*, 186.
152. *The Climate of Monastic Prayer*, 27–28.

The Nature and Meaning of Love

This can be considered Merton's final, definitive vision of the Cistercian vocation in the modern world. In an important way, it would seem to reformulate the Cistercian ideal as it must be lived out in every age of the Church's course here on earth. We know from history that the insights of the Gospels and the New Testament as a whole look past the surface of life into the depths where the human person stands alone, solitary before the judgment of God and is met there by an offer of mercy. The price of receiving that offer is nothing other than the cross of Jesus with the humiliation of seeming defeat and consequent temptation to discouragement. At the same time, Christian hope is the fruit of the resurrection. The Risen Christ has promised his constant presence and support in the form of the Paraclete. In this context Merton presents contemplation as the most effective and honest way of attaining to authenticity of life. But it is not merely a comforting insight into the mystery of God. It is a participation in the agony and anguish of soul that Jesus knew in his Passion. It is a fresh discovery of the true nature of love and of the requirements of fidelity to that love.

Here, then, in this first chapter of his book on the monastic climate of prayer, the three concepts spoken of earlier—contemplation, love, and transformation—reappear in a form that depicts the reality they paint in fresh colors. They define the Cistercian vocation in light of the signs of the times in which Merton lived and which are still actively operative in this beginning phase of the new world culture.

Merton was thoroughly convinced that the fundamental attitude of the monk and, indeed of every Christian, should be openness to the new creation that takes place under the influence of the Holy Spirit. He had written on this topic at various times, and again made it the subject of an essay he published in 1965 under the title *Rebirth and the New Man in Christianity*. In this article he expresses his opinion that the commonly held static view that we gain happiness in the next world as a reward for doing good now is so limited a view of Christianity as to be a serious obstacle to spiritual growth. The real task of the Christian is "the renewal of the self, the 'new creation' in

Christ."[153] He goes on to elaborate his views with considerable feeling.

> The idea of "new birth" is at the very heart of Christianity, and has consequences of profound importance. If this is forgotten—as it so often is—then not only the individual Christian believer but also the Christian community and the society which has traditionally been regarded as Christian all become involved in inner contradictions which eventually lead to crisis.[154]

The reason that this new birth is so essential is that there is no other adequate answer to the problems and mysteries posed by the human condition and the nature of man himself.

Merton's understanding of what this entailed was subject repeatedly to revision as he grew in experience. He considered it a major challenge of church renewal to make the faithful aware of this perspective which radically influences the way one perceives the whole of life. The concept of conversion as a true *metanoia*, which is central in the Gospels, entails this dynamic movement into a future where the unknown is not only the events and situations that will emerge but even one's very self. At this point faith alone provides the light. This is the way that Fr. Louis considered the best suited for the fullness of Christian living, for it alone engages us at the center of our being, from which all the dimensions of our life arise.

In describing this rebirth, Fr. Louis makes the significant point that this rebirth in Christ is not only beyond egoism and selfishness; it is also beyond individuality. It means living for God's glory and for others.

> To be born of the spirit is to be born into God . . . beyond hatred, beyond struggle, in peace, love, joy, self-effacement, service, gentleness, humility, strength.[155]

He realizes that this does not happen all at once, following upon baptism which bestows the Spirit, but requires what he

---

153. Thomas Merton, *Love and Living*, edited by Naomi Burton Stone and Brother Patrick Hart, ocso (New York: Farrar, Straus & Giroux, 1979) 192.
154. Ibid., 193.
155. Ibid., 198.

calls "a continuous dynamic of inner renewal." It entails passing through many stages on the way to completion of the new creature. He envisages this process as culminating in a fullness of love.

> The true Christian rebirth is a renewed transformation, a "passover" in which man is progressively liberated from selfishness and not only grows in love but in some sense "becomes love." The perfection of the new birth is reached where there is no more selfishness, there is only love. In the language of the mystics, there is only Christ; self no longer acts, only the Spirit acts in pure love.[156]

This state of maturity is perhaps not attainable in this life, for any long period at any rate. Certainly any number of mystics have experienced it, but as Saint Bernard put it, such a state is a *rara hora et parva mora* (a rare hour and a short period). Many, like Nicodemus had done when he spoke with our Lord himself about this rebirth, in every age fail to comprehend that this is the very meaning of Christianity. The truly Christian acts of mercy, education, and apostolic undertakings are not merely external acts among others in society; rather they are meant to be the outward expression of this inner life given in the rebirth that comes from above.

Merton understood that there is a great deal of will-to-power in the Western concept of outward, versus inner, work. The love of action and domination that have so long characterized the West all too frequently represent a substitute for this spiritual transformation in view of arriving at perfect love, in a total illumination of the spirit. Without leaving off the laudable commitment to the active apostolate, the authentic Christian must turn his energies to this great inner work that Jesus taught to be essential for salvation. "Unless a man be born again he cannot see the Kingdom of God" (John 3:5).

Certainly, one of the functions of the Cistercian life in our modern world is to keep this interior reality alive and to be a sign of its presence in our time and in our Western society. Because Eastern peoples more readily appreciate this spiritual

156. Ibid., 199.

dimension of life, those who make contemplation and the way of transformation a serious feature of their lifestyle are in a good position to dialogue with them and spread a truer understanding of our Catholic and Cistercian heritage. Merton was a pioneer in this field. His ability to communicate at the level of deep spiritual experience was recognized and appreciated by some of the best representatives of the Buddhist tradition today. Because he was so fully persuaded of the need to cultivate the contemplative dimension of the Christian life Fr. Louis continued to explore it from its many aspects right up to the time of his sudden death.

In 1965 he published a book that has been but little discussed in which he set out perhaps his most full treatment on the theme of love. The title of this work is *Love and Living*, and the most insightful chapter, and the one that expresses the greatest depth of feeling has the catchy title "Love and Need: Is Love a Package or a Message?" He makes the point, first of all, that the attitude one takes to love proves to be the same as that assumed before life itself. Our attitude toward love, revealed by the way we speak of it, is a mixture of fascination, fear, awe, and confusion. For love is a force that takes a person out of himself; he loses control of his life to the extent that he is led by love. It interferes with other interests that may have been more important than anything else in one's past. For love is invasive of the whole person. We are made for others, for the absolute Other in the end, and love achieves the purpose of our being alive when it is accepted and followed with the whole heart.

Love, then, is an issue that everyone must face sooner or later if he is to move ahead in his life. For, as Merton puts it, "love is not just something that happens to you: *it is a certain way of being alive.*" He teases out the implications of this statement in a fullness of analysis that makes his thought more perspicuous and accessible.

> Love is, in fact, an intensification of life, a completeness, a fullness, a wholeness of life. . . . life is not a straight horizontal line between two points, birth and death. Life curves upward to a peak of intensity, a high point of value and meaning, at which all its latent creative possibilities go into

action and the person transcends himself or herself in encounter, response and communion with another. It is for this that we came into the world—this communion and self-transcendence. We do not become fully human until we give ourselves to each other in love. And this must not be confined only to sexual fulfillment: it embraces everything in the human person—the capacity for self-giving, for sharing, for creativity, for mutual care, for spiritual concern.[157]

Obviously, Merton here is considering love in its human dimension and expression, not divine love as such. In the course of this article, in fact, he does not mention contemplation or prayer. He does not have to as he is grounded, as I have said before, in the Cistercian tradition that grasps that whatever is said concerning human love is implicated in the process of transformation of love from carnal to divine. Understanding the inner relatedness of human love to the love of God is a condition for the discovery of the true self. It also conditions the effective collaboration with the grace of God in the endeavor to achieve the aim of life, the renewal of the inner self in the image of God.

1965, the year Merton wrote *Love and Living*, marked the beginning of Merton's life as a hermit. He had earlier been spending half a day in the hermitage. Now he was freed from his position as novice-master and moved from the monastery to the nearby woods where a plain, cement block building served as his cell. In May of that same year he described in an essay his daily routine, with reflections and comments which he expressed in language that rises to poetic intensity, his way of understanding his new lifestyle, with its large dosage of silence and solitude. He makes a connection between these practices and human love that explicitly reveals how he understood the relationship of these realities, which, in the opinion of most people, are seemingly unconnected.

> One might say I had decided to marry the silence of the forest. The sweet dark warmth of the whole world will have to be my wife. Out of the heart of that dark warmth comes the secret that is heard only in silence, but it is at the root

---

157. *Love and Living*, 27.

of all the secrets that are whispered by all the lovers in their beds all over the world. So perhaps I have an obligation to preserve the stillness, the silence, the poverty, the virginal point of pure nothingness which is at the center of all other loves. I attempt to cultivate this plant without comment in the middle of the night and water it with psalms and prophecies in silence.[158]

As he pursued his reflections on this theme, he spoke with deepening conviction concerning the irreplaceable experience of self-giving in love as a condition for the discovery of the true self and so as essential for a true contemplative life. Without a personal, self-transcending, and committed love, life loses its real meaning and seriousness. "For," he writes,

> love is our true destiny. We do not find the meaning of life by ourselves alone—we find it with another. We do not discover the secret of our lives merely by study and calculation in our own isolated meditations. The meaning of our life is a secret that has to be revealed to us in love, *by the one we love*. And if this love is unreal, the secret will not be found. . . . We will never be fully real until we let ourselves fall in love—either with another human person or with God.[159]

St. Aelred, as novice-master, had examined in fastidious detail the various qualities and motivations of love in his *Mirror of Charity*. He becomes very concrete in his treatment in Book III where he analyzes all the varied mixtures of affection, attachment, self-interest, and selflessness that make the reality of human love so fascinating and mysterious. He takes such pains because he is keenly aware of the ease with which deception falsifies true love and frustrates its proper effects and purposes. Wiser, more experienced, and still fully convinced of the primacy of love and friendship when he became abbot, one of his first undertakings was to begin writing his treatise *On Friendship*. A careful reading of this work reveals how highly such friend-

---

158. Thomas Merton, *Day of A Stranger*. Introduction by Robert E. Daggy (Salt Lake City: Gibbs M. Smith, Inc., 1981) 49.
159. *Love and Living*, 27.

ship as he describes is to be valued, and at the same time, how very exacting are the conditions for establishing and maintaining such a relationship over an extended period of time. The elusiveness of human motivation in the concrete are nowhere more present than in human love and friendship, for the whole person is engaged at all levels of being, including the unconscious and preconscious. St. Aelred took such pains to describe the aberrations and distortions of love, as well as its genuine expression, precisely because he treasured the genuine form so highly.

Merton, perhaps unconsciously, followed in the same tradition, imbued as he was with the same spirit of the Cistercian Fathers. He carried out, in his personal manner, the same program in the course of this article. He described in some detail the ways in which modern culture falsifies love's true nature and so frustrates its possibilities for spiritual creativity. His analysis of technological society is intended to serve the same purpose as the Abbot of Rievaulx had in mind in his writings: to mirror the distorted forms of personal relations so as to enable recognition of its true visage.

> We consciously or unconsciously tailor our notions of love according to the patterns that we are exposed to day after day in advertising, in movies, on TV, and in our reading. One of these prevailing ready-made attitudes toward life and love needs to be discussed here. It is one that is seldom consciously spelled out. It is just "in the air". . . Love is regarded as a deal. . . . We unconsciously think of ourselves as objects for sale in the market. We do not give ourselves in love, we make a deal that will enhance our own product, and therefore no deal is final.[160]

His further analysis of this attitude to human relations throws light on a number of characteristics of our contemporaries, more strikingly a source of unrest today than when Merton wrote these lines: the difficulty in making definitive commitments. The alarmingly increasing rate of divorce and the frequency of dispensation from priesthood and solemn vows attest to the gravity of this weakness, which is, fundamentally, a failure

160. Ibid., 29.

to love. Merton points out that love is not essentially the fulfillment of needs; it is not, in its tendency, self-fulfillment. For love is not a lack, a void that can be exploited, he notes. On the contrary, it is a unique force, a power that is creative and life giving.

As we come to the end of our reflections on Merton's contributions to renewal of the Cistercian tradition in light of the signs of the times, let us draw upon a citation of his own concept of what true love, in all its forms, is in its nature. In my opinion this is one of the most eloquent and moving passages in all of Merton's oeuvre, and perhaps the one that displays more vividly than any others his affinity with the early Cistercian Fathers, and at the same time, his ability to translate and elaborate upon their teachings for the people of our times.

> Love is the revelation of our deepest personal meaning, value and identity. . . . Love, then, is a transforming power of almost mystical intensity that endows the lovers with qualities and capacities they never dreamed they could possess. Where do these qualities come from? From the enhancement of life itself, deepened, intensified, elevated, strengthened, and spiritualized by love. Love is not only a special way of being alive, it is the perfection of life. He who loves is more alive and more real than he was when he did not love. . . Life looks completely different to him and all his values change.[161]

Fr. Louis closed one of his works on contemplation with a citation from the highly cultivated and contemplative Clement of Alexandria. Let it serve to close this book. It makes explicit the dominant spirit in which he presented his own inner life and thought to the monks and nuns of our Order, and to the modern world.

> Bound to the wood of a cross, thou art free from all danger of destruction. God's Logos will steer thy ship and the Holy Pneuma or the Holy Spirit will give thee a safe return to heaven's harbor.[162]

161. Ibid., 35–36.
162. Thomas Merton, *Contemplation in a World of Action* (Notre Dame, IN: Notre Dame University Press, 1998) 226.

ACKNOWLEDGMENTS

The author gratefully acknowledges the following publishers for permission to use material from their publications:

FARRAR, STRAUS AND GIROUX, LLC

Excerpts from LOVE AND LIVING by Thomas Merton. Copyright © 1956 by the Abbey of Our Lady of Gethesemani, Inc. Copyright renewed 1984 by Trustees of the Thomas Merton Legacy Trust. Excerpts from THE SCHOOL OF CHARITY by Thomas Merton, edited by Brother Patrick Hart. Copyright © 1990 by the Merton Legacy Trust.

NEW DIRECTIONS PUBLISHING CORPORATION

By Thomas Merton, from THE WAY OF CHUANG TZU, copyright © 1965 by The Abbey of Gethsemani. Reprinted by permission of New Directions Publishing Corp.

INDEX

Abbaye de Melleraye, vii
Abbey of the Genesee, viii, 33, 45, 52
Abbey of Gethsemani, viii, x, 5, 32, 36, 54, 64
Abbey of St. Joseph (Spencer), iv
Abbot General (Dom Gabriel Sortais), 8, 9, 21, 22, 29, 36
Abbot of Monastery of the Holy Spirit, 35
Adams, Henry, 27
Aelred of Rievaulx, 87, 95, 99, 124, 125
Alberic, Saint, 23
American culture, 14
apex of the soul, 92, 104, 124
Apophtegmata Patrum (Sayings of the Fathers), 17, 89
Apostolic Delegate, 21
Arsenius, 73
Ascent to Truth, The, 3 n. 4, 58, 59
asceticism, 65, 98, 99
Asian Journal of Thomas Merton, The, 18
Athanasius, 76
Augustine, Saint, 2, 34, 35, 46, 59, 65, 75, 91, 92

Baldwin, Abbot of Ford, 115
Balthasar, Hans Urs von, 12
Bamberger, John Eudes, Abbot, vii–xii, 33
Basic Principles of Monastic Spirituality, 56
Basil, Saint, 17, 46
Benedict, Saint, 65
Benedictines, 39
Bennett, Dr. Tom, 23
Bernard, Saint, Abbot of Clairvaux, 2, 13, 17, 38, 46, 51, 55, 59, 65, 71, 86, 87, 95, 96, 98, 99, 115
Bible, 76
Blake, William, 27, 28
Bonaventure, St., 115
Book of Life, xi, 7
Bramachari, 63, 64

Camus, 26, 27
cargo cults, 81
Carmelites, 39
Cassian, John, 43, 44, 55, 57, 58, 65, 71
censors, 8, 22, 29
Christ, *see* Jesus

Chuang Tzu, 66, 75
Cistercian, ix, 18, 19, 51, 68, 71, 88
Cistercian Fathers, 33, 34, 99,125
  renewal, xii, 63
  tradition, vii–ix, 20, 39, 40, 43, 53, 57, 67, 94, 110,122
  vocation, xi, 119
City of God, 65
civil rights, 4
Clement of Alexandria, 126
Climate of Monastic Prayer, The, 69, 116, 118
Collected Poems of Thomas Merton, The, 18, 106
Confessions, 63
Confucius, 60, 66
Conjectures of a Guilty Bystander, 6, 82
Constitutions, 54
Contemplation, viii, ix, 40, 52, 54–57, 63, 66–68, 75, 77–85, 90, 94, 100, 103, 104, 109–111, 116, 118, 119
Contemplation in a World of Action, 126
Contemplative life, ix, 56, 60, 111–113, 116
Contemplative Prayer, 70
conversion, 120
Courage for Truth, The, 82
culture, 54, 60, 61, 112, 125
Cyril of Alexandria, Saint, 34, 35

Dalai Lama, 61, 63
Dancing in the Water of Life, 6, 24, 32, 70
Dante, 65
Day of a Stranger, 124
Deseilles, P. Placide, 38, 39, 54
Desert Fathers, 17, 44, 65, 71
diversion, 59

Divine Office, 52
divinization, 53, 76, 101
Dunn, Susan, 7

Eckhart, Meister, 62
Eichrodt, Walter, 2
Elizabeth of the Trinity, 12
Entering the Silence: Becoming A Monk and Writer, 3 n.3, 4, 6, 29, 32, 100
Erasmus, 24
Evagrius (Ponticus), xi, 55, 72
  Praktikos, 72
Exile Ends in Glory, 3 n.2

faith, 49
false self, 90, 94, 101–103, 116
Fathers of the Church, 34, 35, 43
Flanagan, Fr. Raymond, 54, 55
formation, monastic, 34–36, 40–42, 60, 96, 111, 112
Foucauld, Charles de, 12
Founders of Cistercians, 23, 38
Fox, Dom James, Abbot, viii, 32, 33, 37
Franciscans, 39
Freud, 82

General Chapter, ix, 33, 49
Giustiniani, Paul, 13
Gregory the Great, Pope, 12, 34, 35
Gregory of Nyssa, xi, 59, 60
grace, 56

Hadewijch, 115
Harding, St. Stephen, 40
Heidegger, 116
hermitage, 36, 37, 123
Hesychasm, 74, 76
Herve, Dom, 42
Hesychia, 74

Higgins, Michael W., 10, 26
Holy Ghost, *see* Spirit of God
Holy Mass, 52
House of Studies, 36
Humanism, 53, 70
Huxley, Aldous, 63

identity, 53, 102, 103
image of God, 86–88, 104
Imitation of Christ, 63
Incarnation, 76
inconsistency, 26, 28
Inner Experience, 74, 82, 90
Isaac of Stela, 99

Jerome, Saint, 13
Jesuits, 39
Jesus Christ, xi, 31, 56, 66, 67, 69, 70, 76, 97, 98, 105, 119–121
John the Baptist, 18 n.26
John of the Cross, 59, 60, 65, 80

Kierkegaard, 116

Leclercq, Jean, osb, 2, 12, 13, 29, 33, 43, 49
lectio, 38, 52
Leo, Saint, Pope, 34, 35
liberum arbitrium, 86, 87
liberum consilium, 87
likeness, 86–88, 100
love, ix, 95, 96, 104, 105, 107, 109, 110, 119, 121, 122, 124, 126
Love and Living, 122
Luther, Martin, 15

Marcel, Gabriel, x
Maritain, Jacques, 63
Maximus the Confessor, 76
McGinn, Bernard, 74
Merton, Thomas (Father Louis), vii–xii, 1 and *passim*
  hermit, 36, 123

junior master (master of scholastics, Magister Spiritus), 41, 43, 83, 85
novice master, viii, 83, 123
poet, vii, 2, 20, 85
prophet, vii, 1, 5, 8, 16 and *passim*
rebel, 19, 20, 22, 23
teacher, 31
writer: artist and style, vii, 4, 5
Molesmes, 23
Monastery of Novo Mundo (Brazil), xi
Monastic Journey, The, 37, 52, 55
Montaldo, Jonathan, xii
Morson, Dom John, 41
Mott, Michael, 23 n 32, 24
mystical theology, 31, 59
mysticism, 54–59, 63, 74, 75, 83

New Man, The, 97
New Seeds of Contemplation, 8 n.17, 79, 82, 83, 94, 101
No Man Is an Island, 85
Norris, Kathleen, 14

Oakam, 19, 23
ordination, 31
Oriental thought, 61, 63, 68, 69
Origen, xi, 59, 113, 114

Patristics, 35
Paul, St. 76, 77
peace, 42
penance, 52
Peter Damian, Saint, 13
poverty, 39
prayer, 38, 49, 73, 74, 93
precariousness, ix
priesthood, 31, 32
prophet and prophecy, 16 and *passim*

Index

psalms, 71
Pseudo-Dionysius, 59
psychiatry, 51

quies (rest), 73, 75, 76

Rahner, Karl, 56, 85
Rance, Armand Jean de, 37, 45
Ratio Studiorum, 42
rebel, 8 ,19, 20, 22
rebirth, 120, 121
reformer, xi, 16 and *passim*
renewal, 63, 120, 126
renunciation, 49
Rilke, x, 26, 27
Roloff, Ronald, osb, 1
Rousseau, Olivier, 39
Rule, 56, 100
Run to the Mountain, 5 n.8, 9

satire, 23, 26
satori, 91
School of Charity, 2 n.1, 3, 8, 9, 11, 20, 28, 33, 118
Scripture, 31
Search for Solitude, 7
Seeds of Contemplation, 6, 8, 79, 82
Seven Storey Mountain (autobiography), 3, 5, 15, 19, 31, 52, 64, 65, 66, 80, 108
Shaker theology, 81
Shannon, Monsignor William, 20 n.28, 75, 80, 81
Sign of Jonas, The, 4, 8
signs of the times, 126
silence, 49, 123, 124
simplicity, 39
solitude, 37, 83, 118, 123
Sortais, Dom Gabriel, *see* Abbot General
Spirit of God, 31, 33, 38, 45, 56, 77, 88, 118–120, 126

Spiritual Directory, 51, 54
spiritual senses, 113–115
Standaert, P. Maur, 42
Statute on Unity and Pluralism, 49
Steere, Douglas, 69
studies, 33, 42
Suzuki, D.T., 63, 66

Tao, 65–68, 76
Tauler, 92, 93
Teresa of Avila, 80
theology, 31, 58
theoria physike, 58, 107
Thèrése of Lisieux, Saint, 12
Thomas Aquinas, 59, 65
Thomas Merton Reader, A, 61
tradition, 43, 44
transcendence, 123
Transfiguration, 97, 98
transformation, ix, 31, 40, 53, 83, 89, 92, 96, 98–101, 103, 105, 107–110, 119, 121
Trappist, 18, 51, 52
Trent, Council of, 47
true self, 53, 76, 77, 83, 86, 89–94, 103, 110, 112, 124
Tugwell, Fr. Simon, op, 74.

unlikeness, 102

Valery-Radot, Irenee, 12
virginal point (*see* apex of soul), 124
Vogue, Adalbert, osb, 2
Vow of Conversation, A: Journals 1964–1965, 28

Way of Chuang Tzu, The, 66
What Are These Wounds?, 3 n.2
What Is Contemplation?, 74, 79, 83
Wilkes, Paul, 80, 81

William of St. Thierry, 17, 71, 95, 99, 114, 115
Wisdom of the Desert, The, 17, 74
Witness to Freedom, 55
word(s), 49, 50, 104
work of the heart, 98

Wu, Dr. John, 67
Wu-wei, 65

Zen and the Birds of Appetite, 62, 67
Zen Buddhism, 59–62, 65–69, 71, 73

Printed in Great Britain
by Amazon